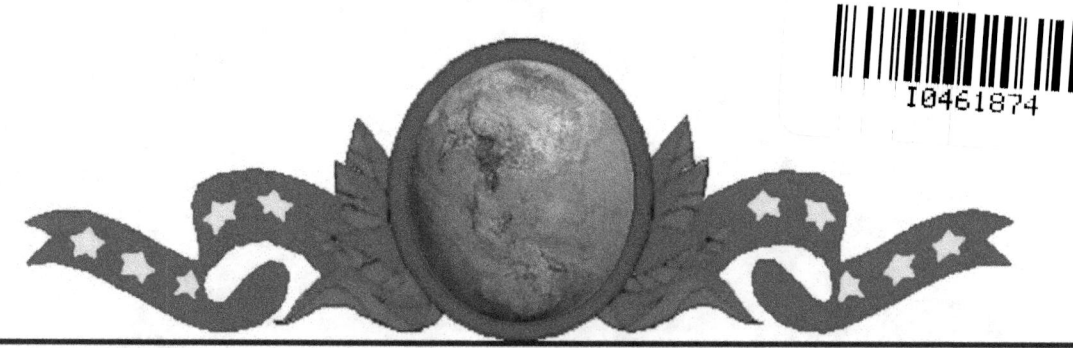

Real World
Colouring Book
For Advanced Users & Adults

50 Images

Created From Real Life Photos
For You To Colour As You Please.

ISBN 978-0-359-78784-5

9 780359 787845

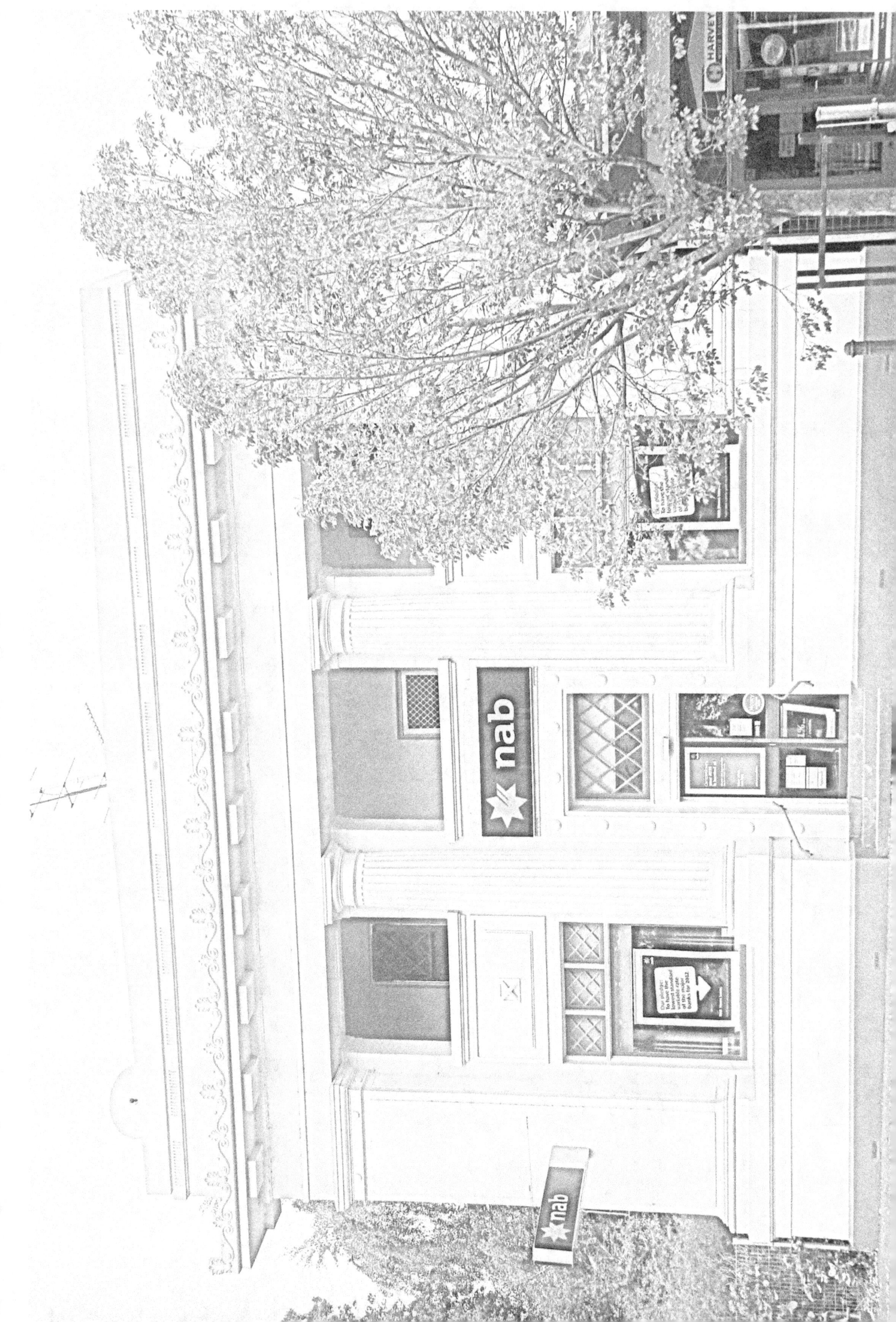

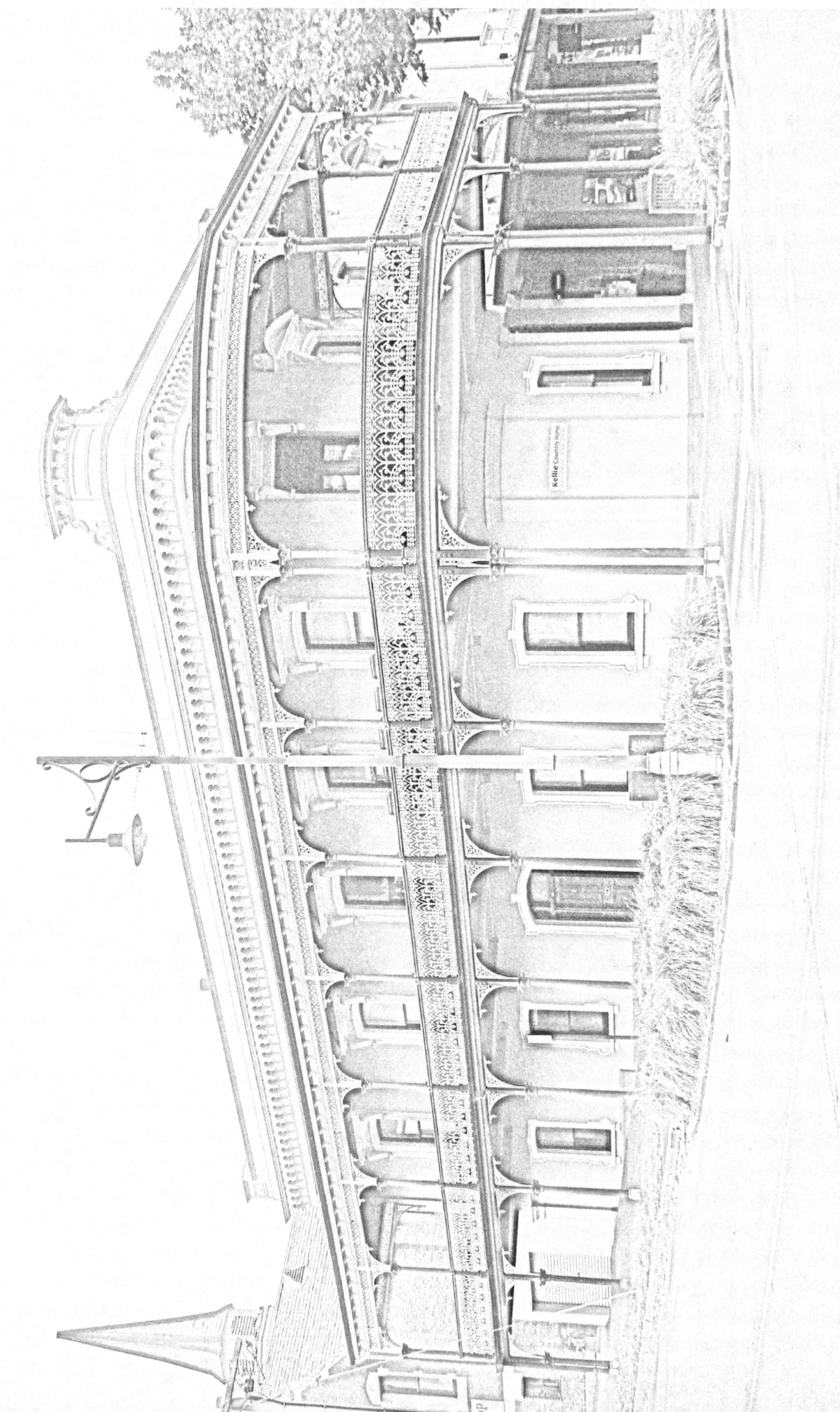

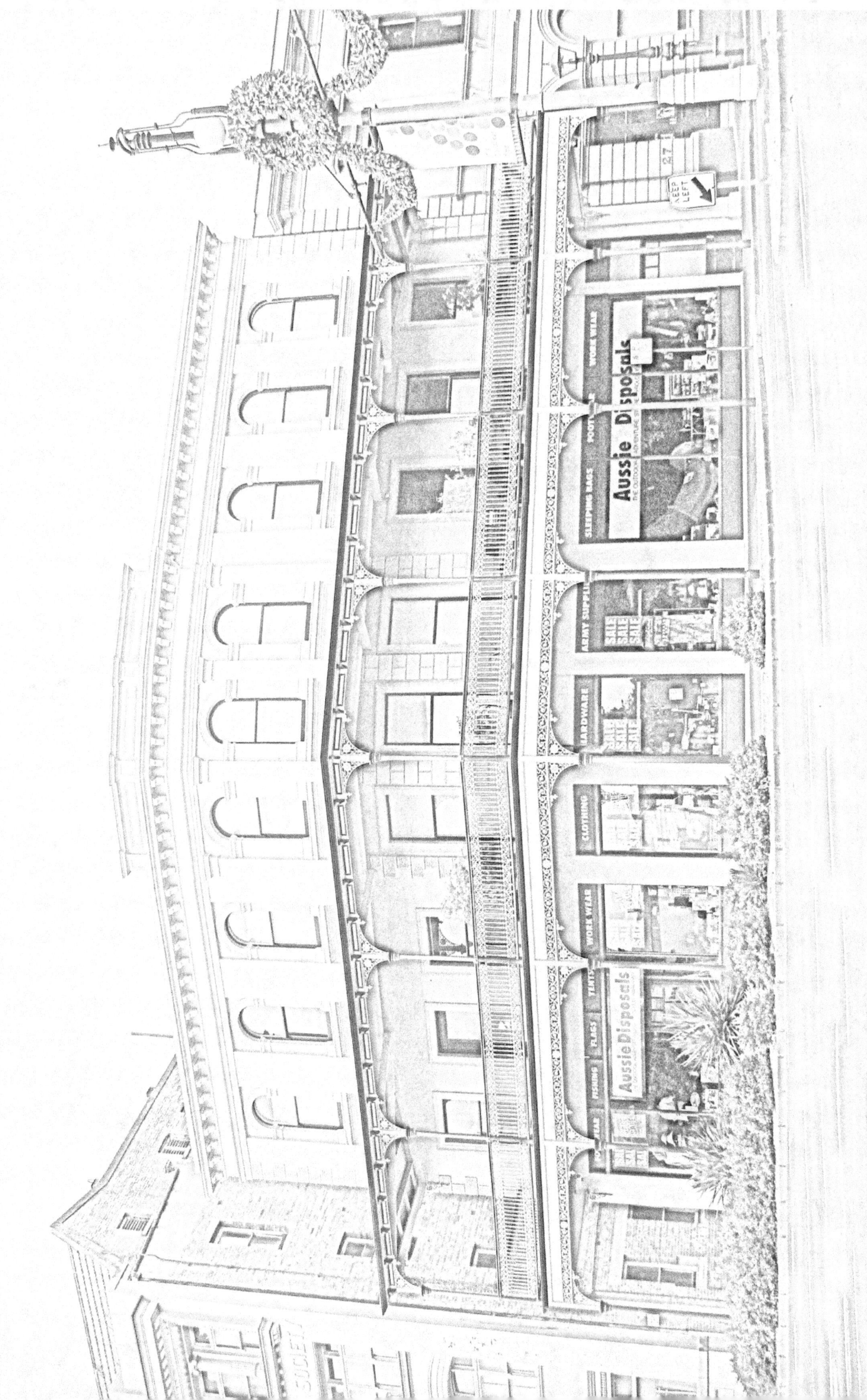

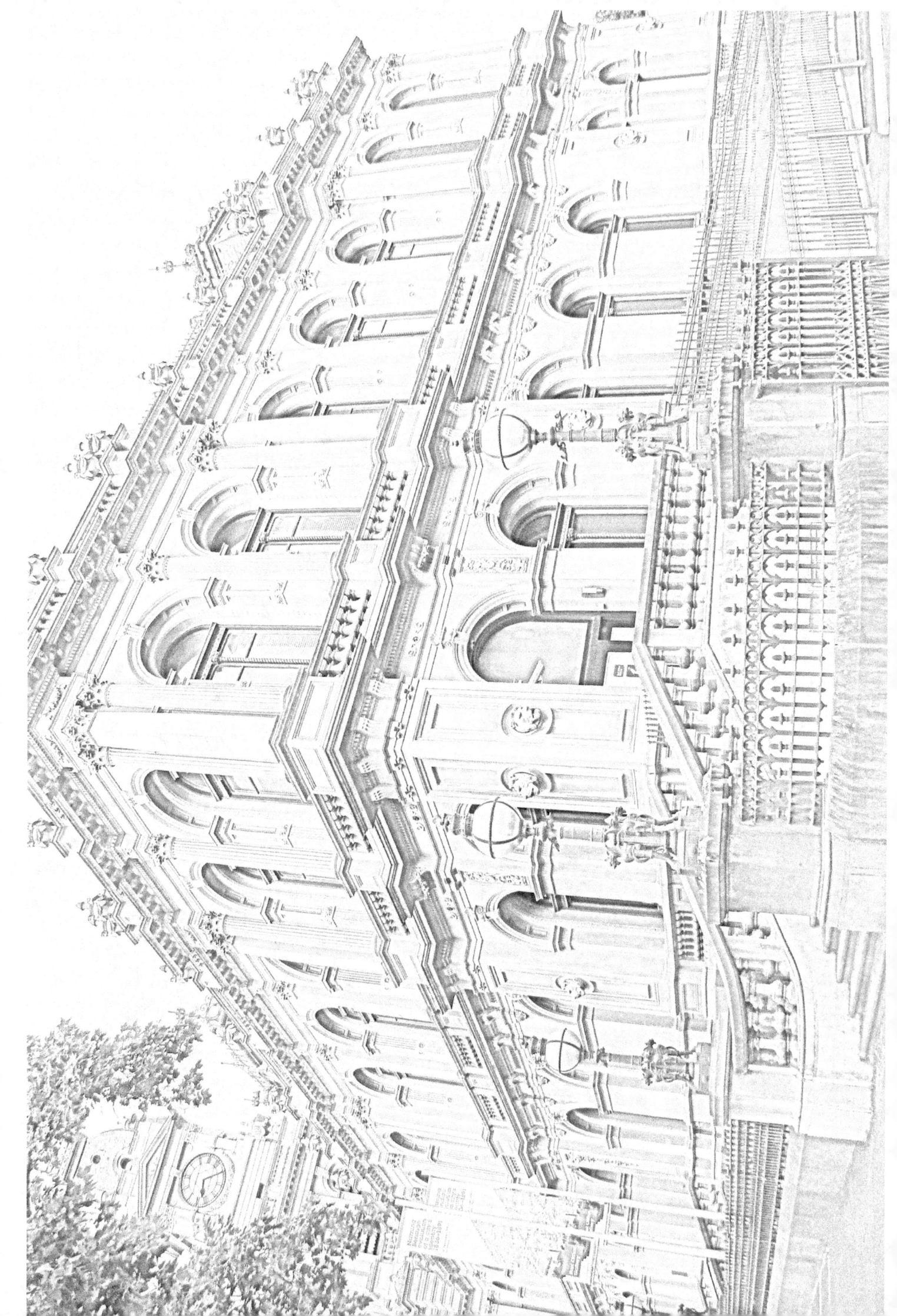

Birds

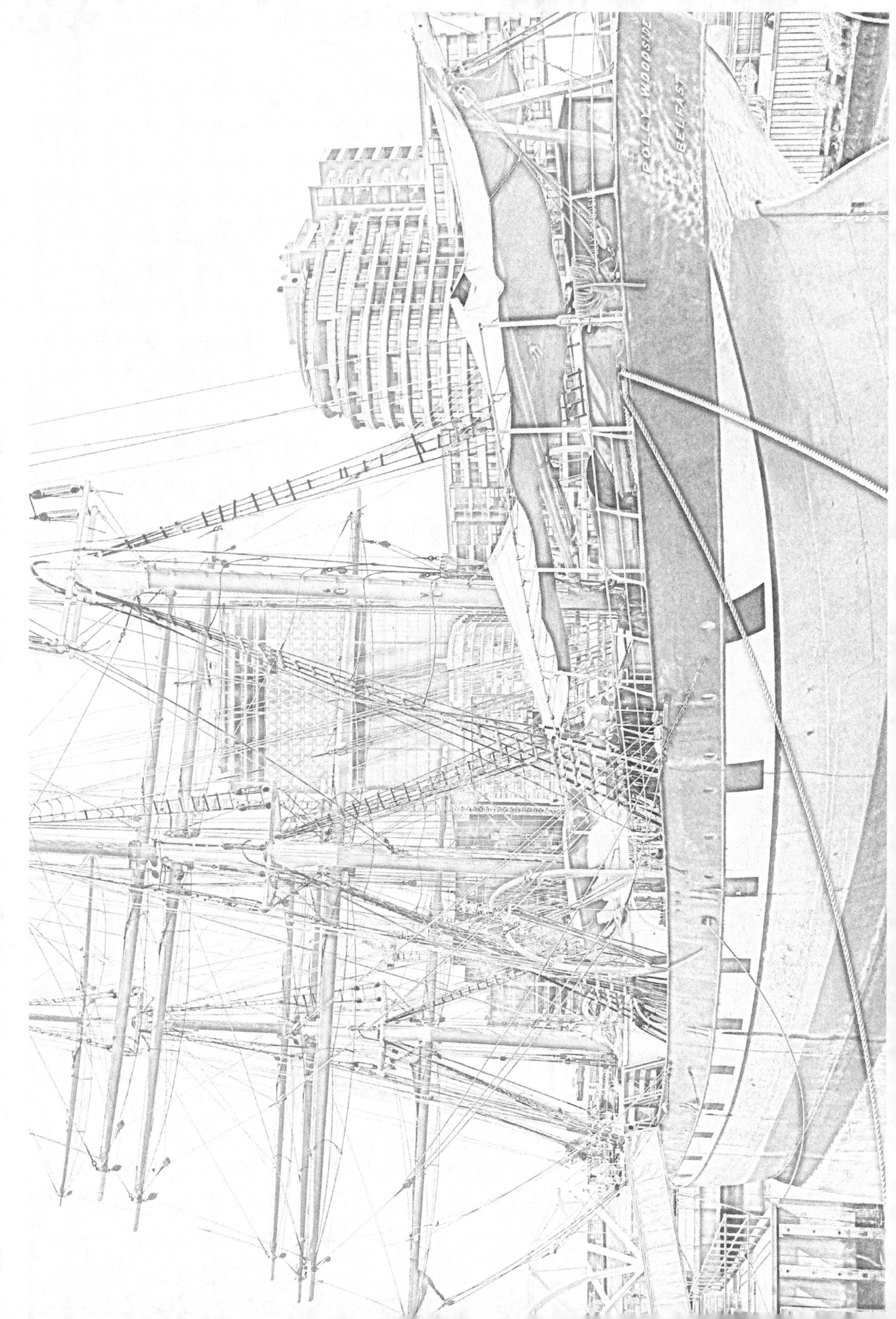

Boats On The Water

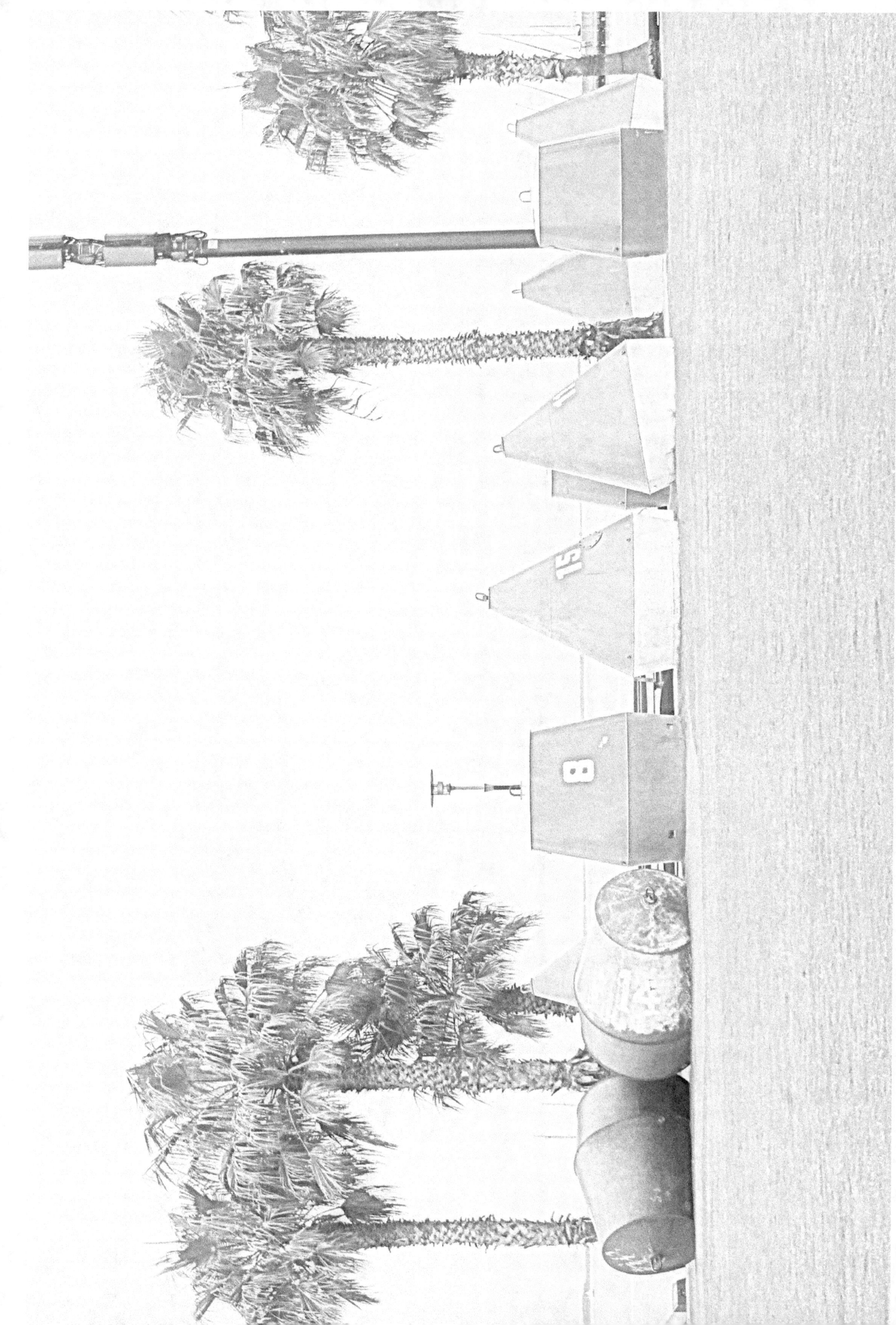

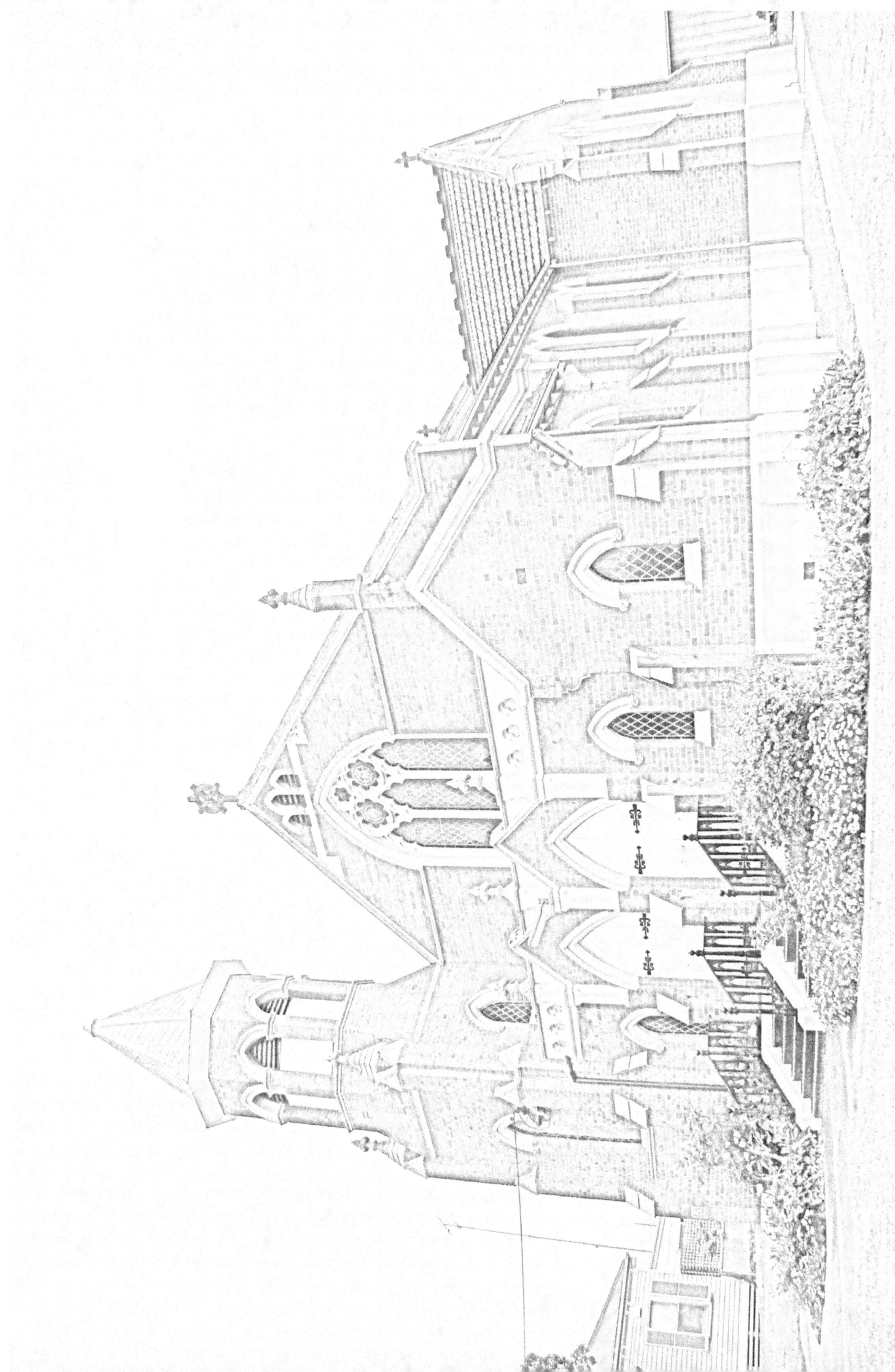

Church

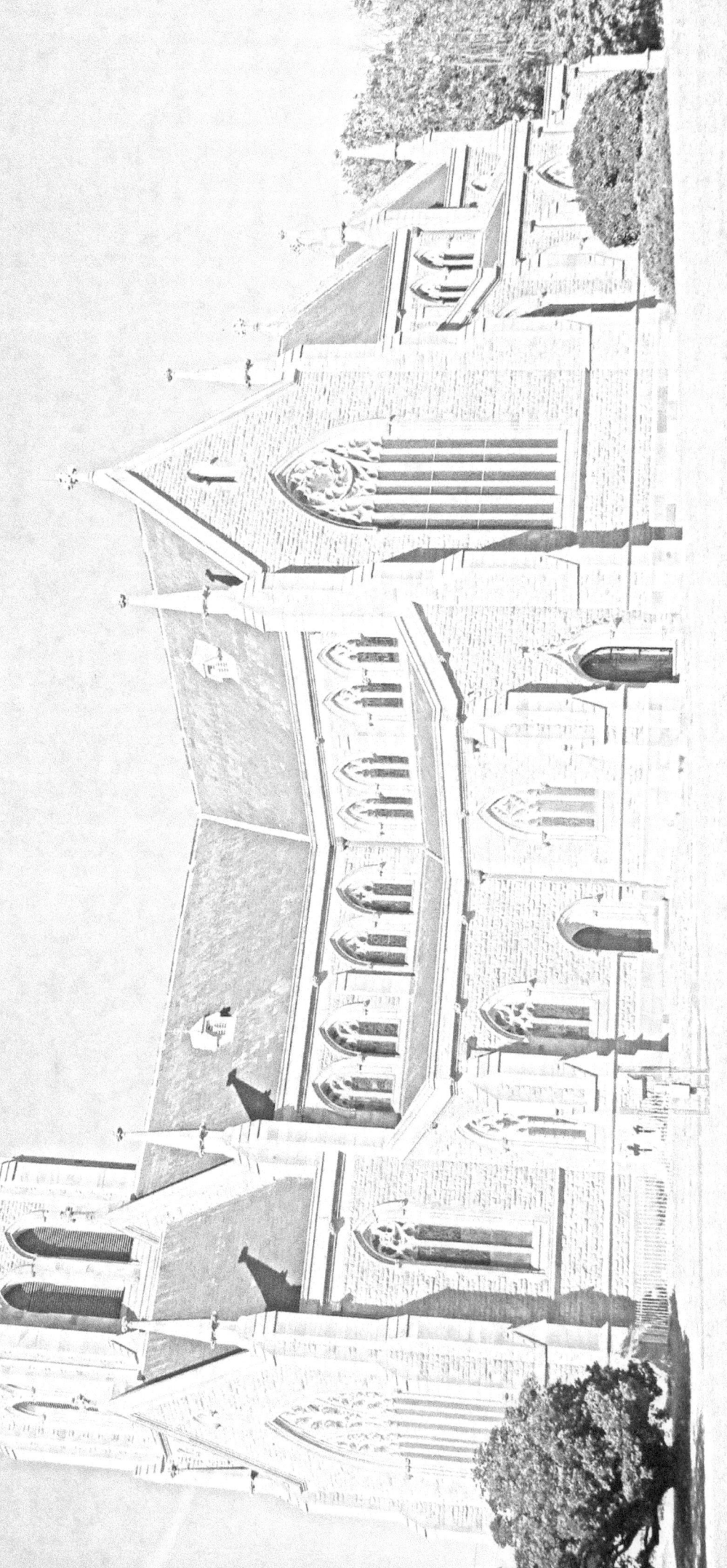

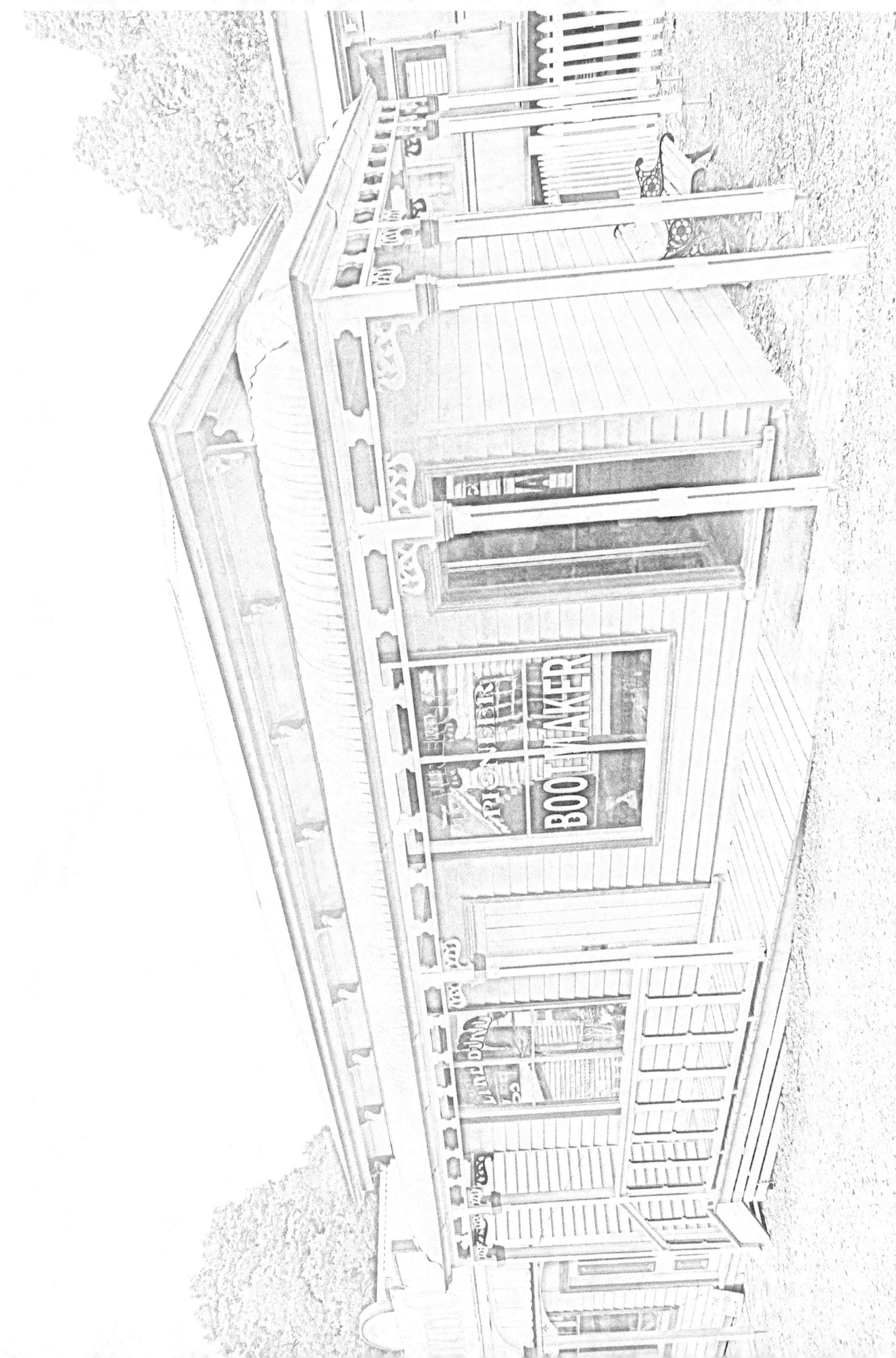

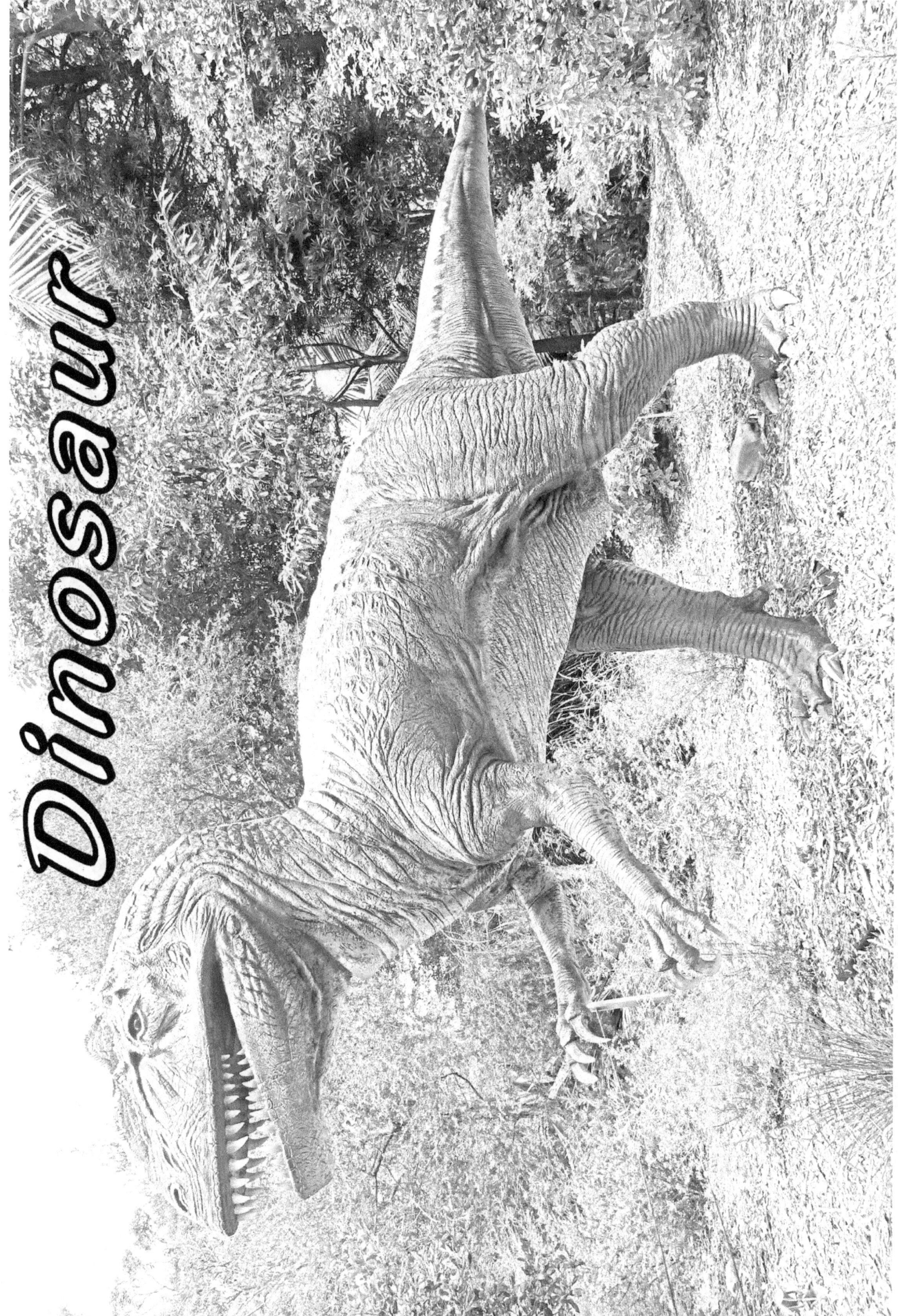

Dinosaur

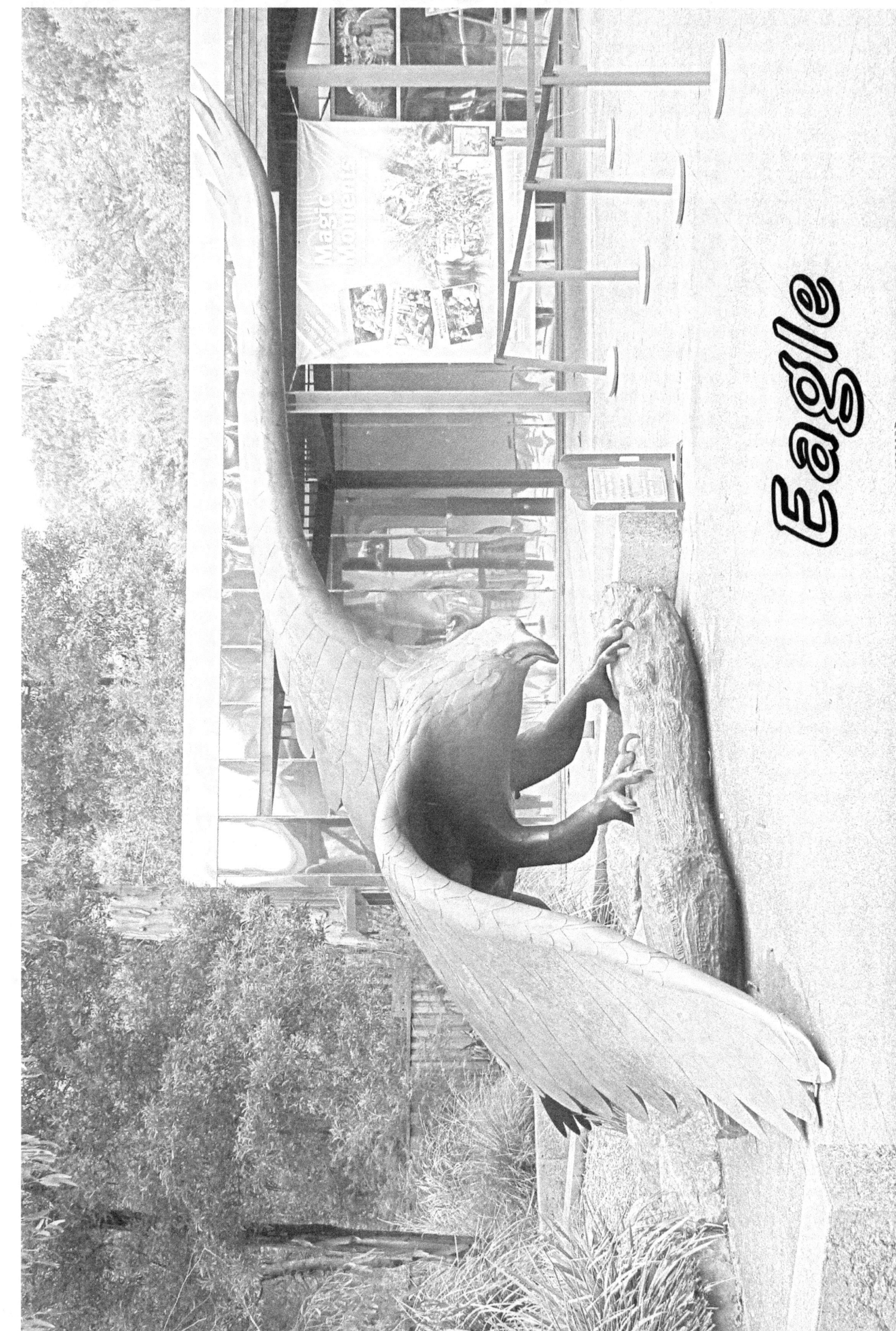

Eagle

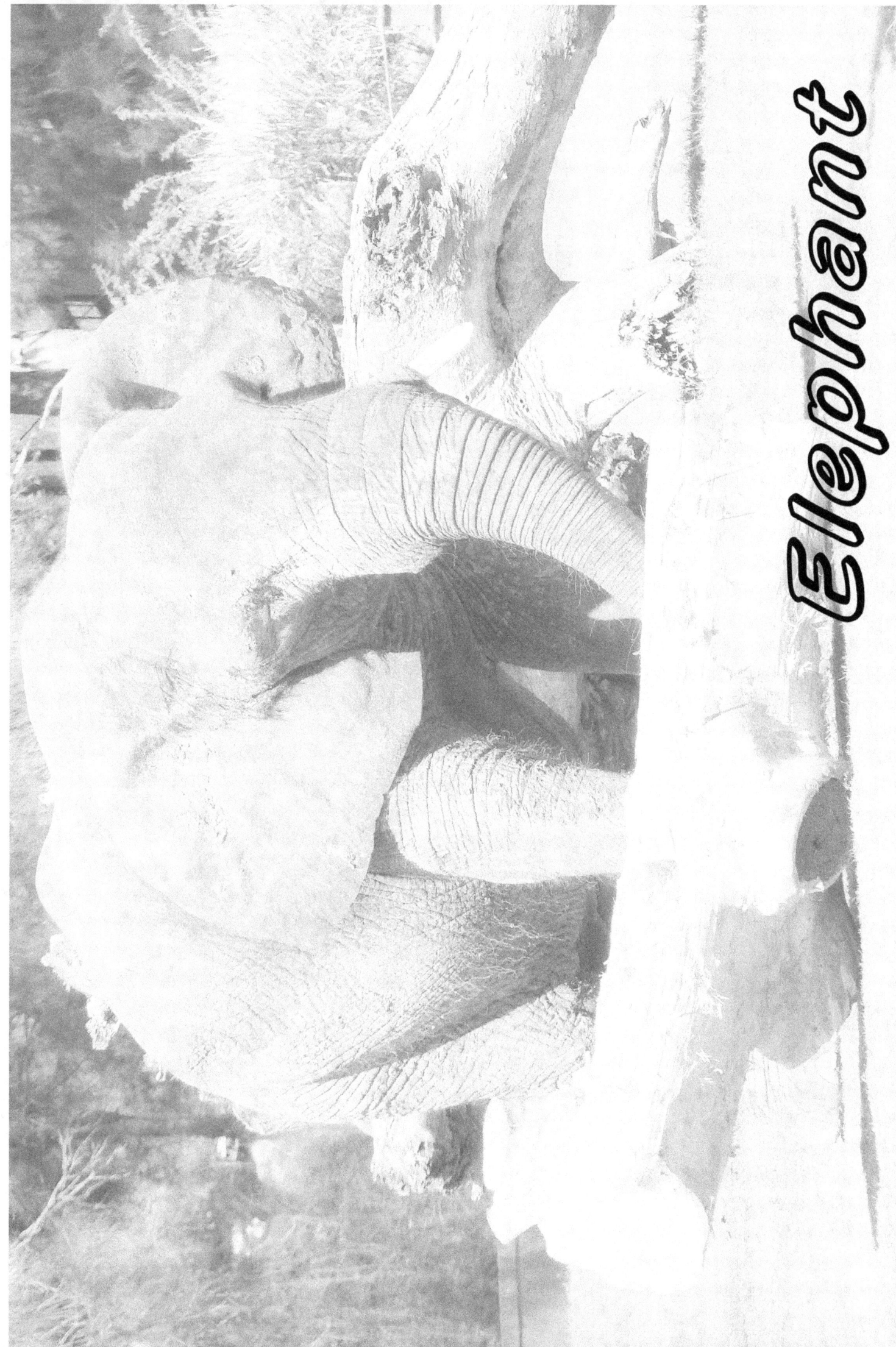

Elephant

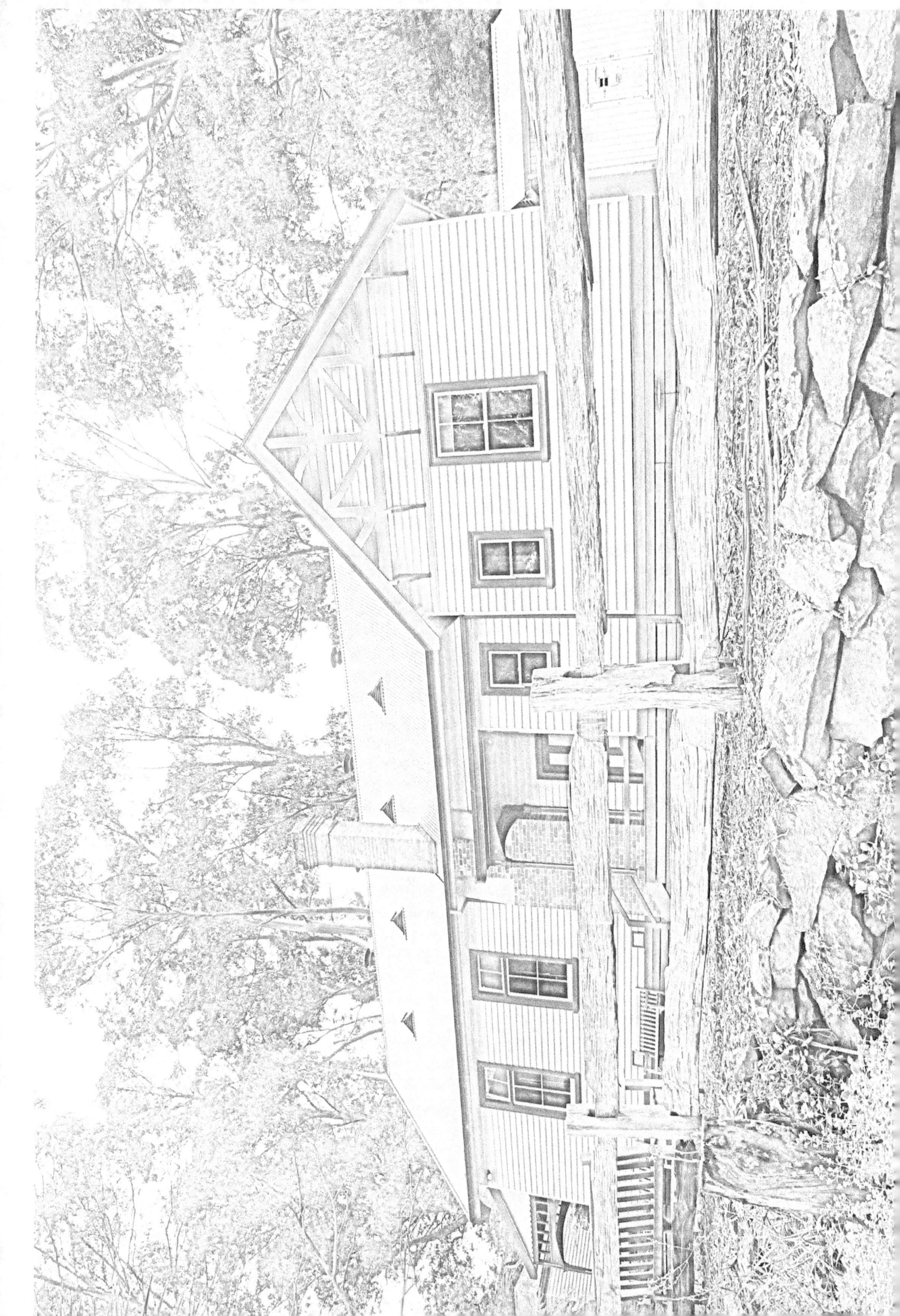

Fire Station

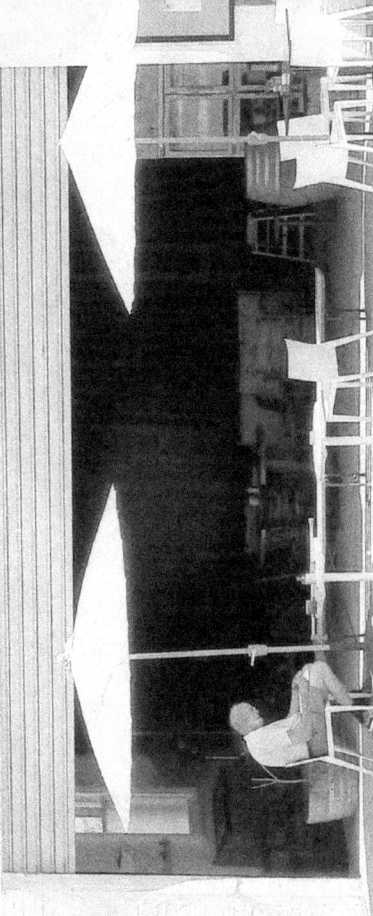

CASTLE MAINE

1906

FIRE BRICADE STATION

C.V.F.B.

DEPOT

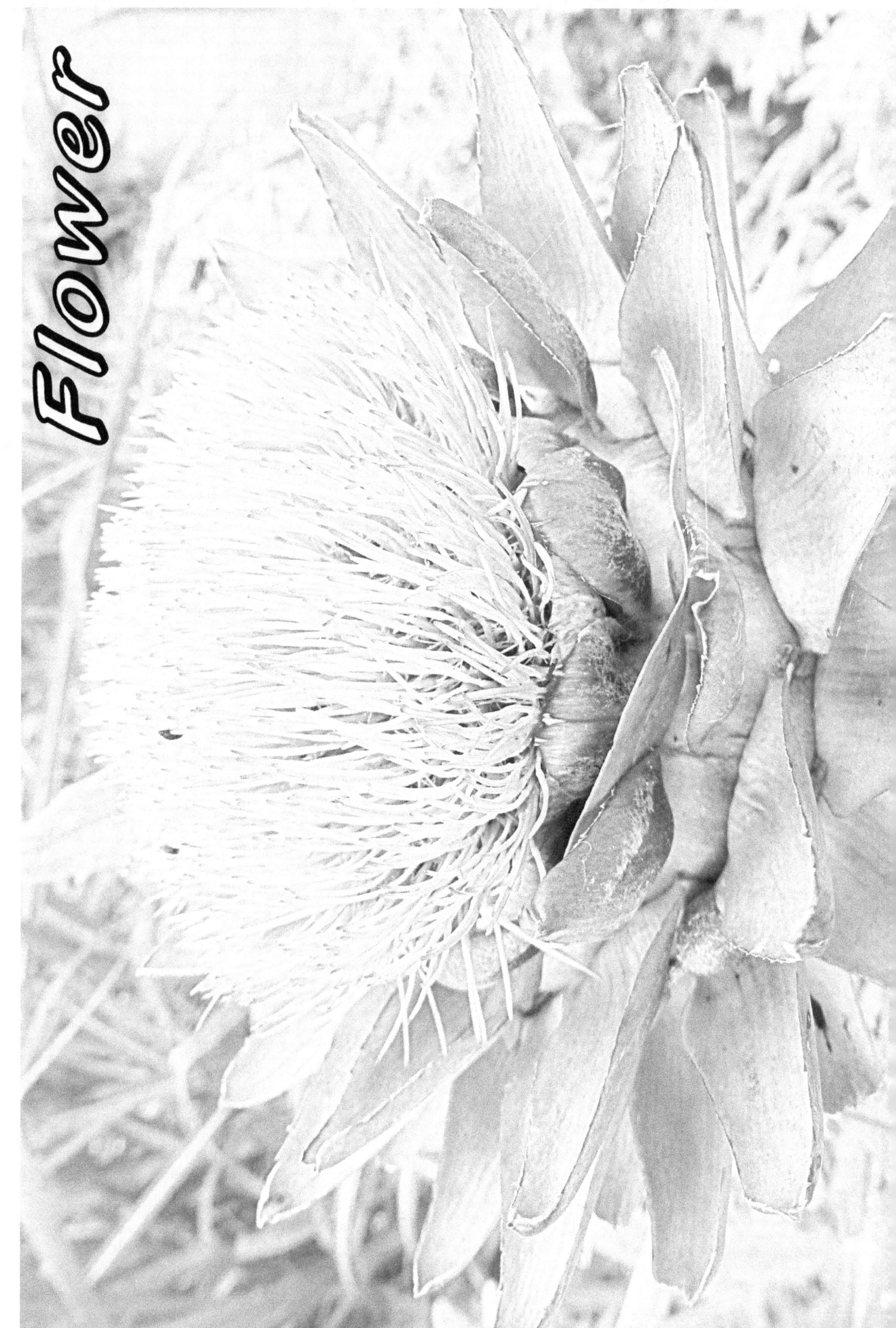

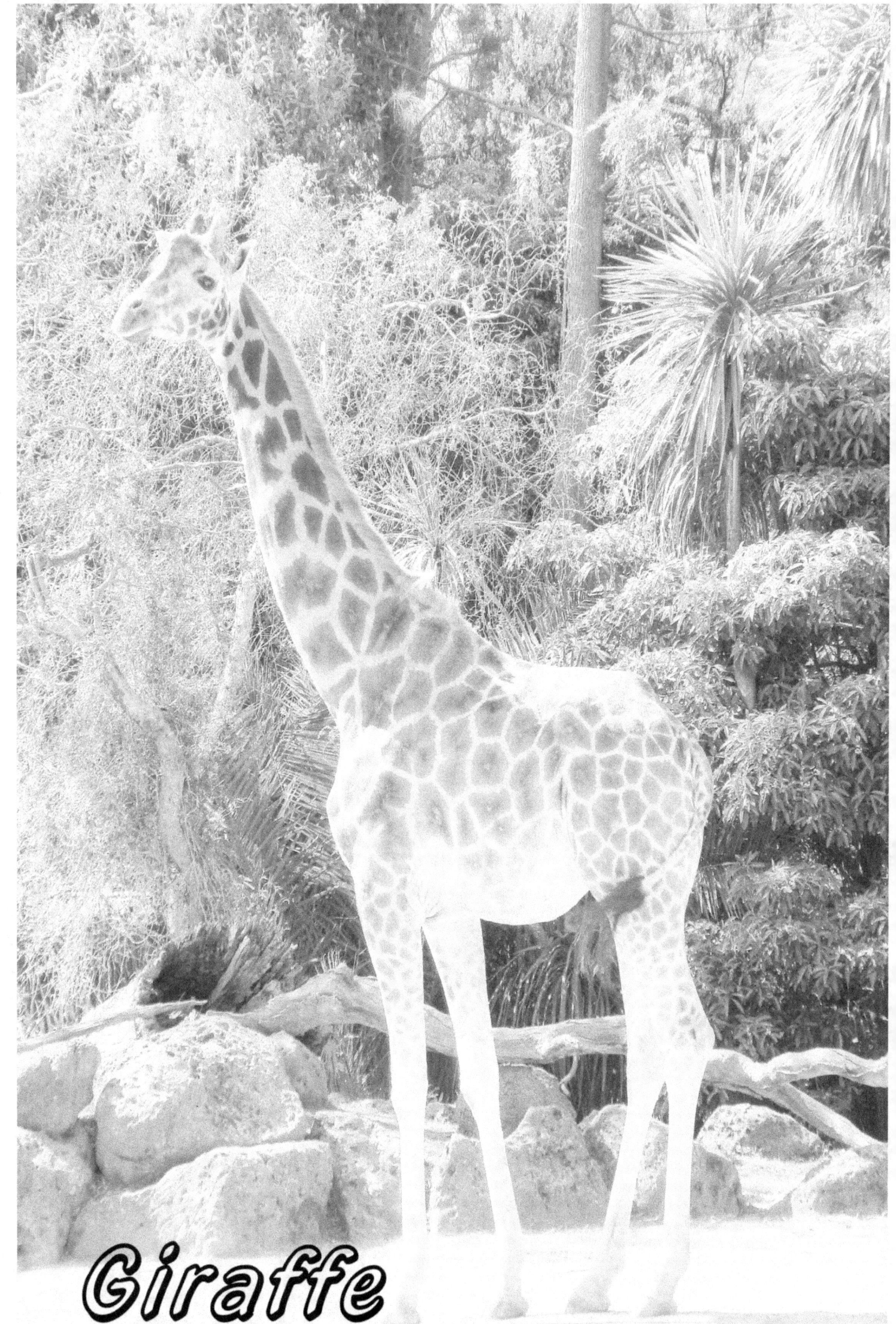

Giraffe

GOOSE

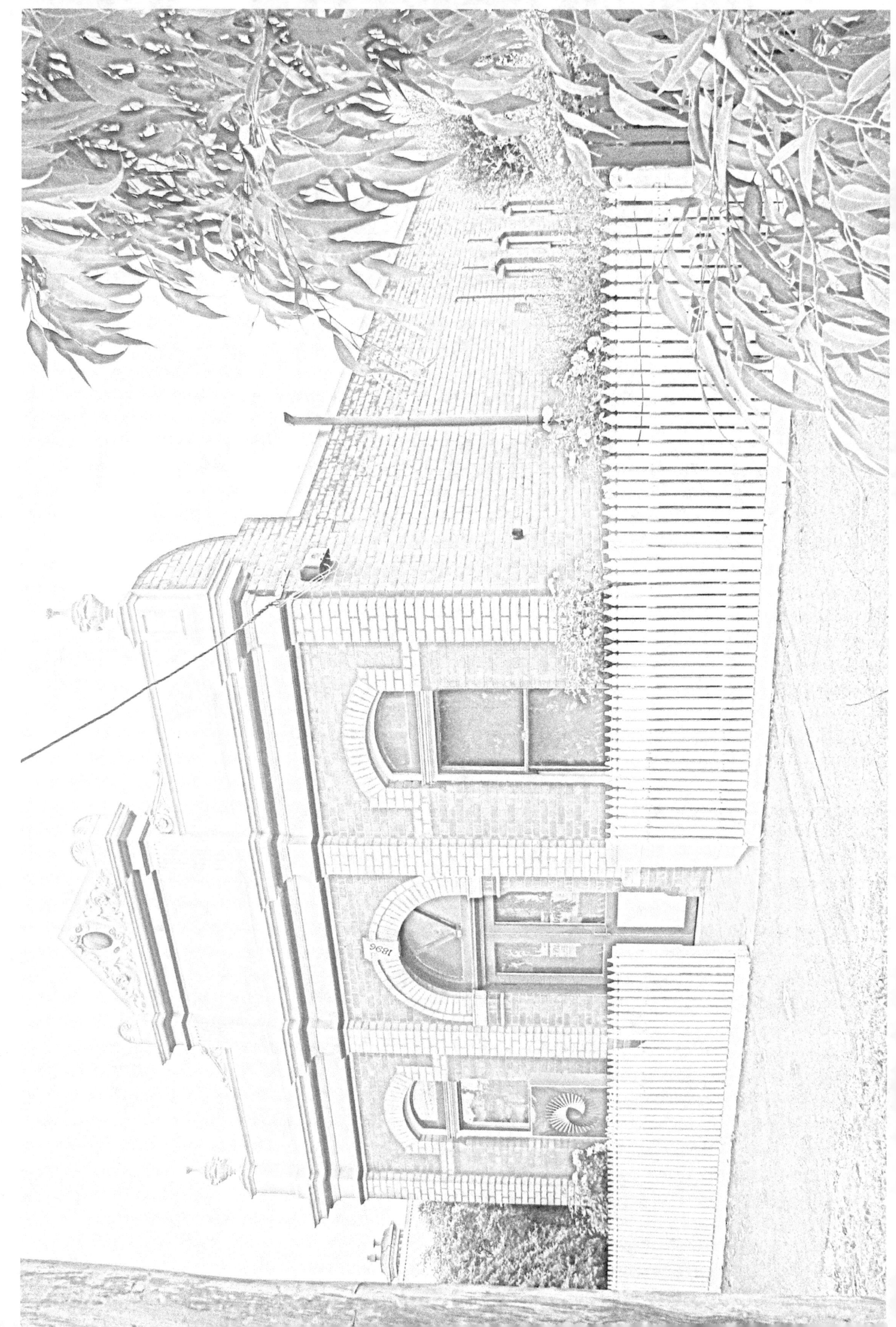

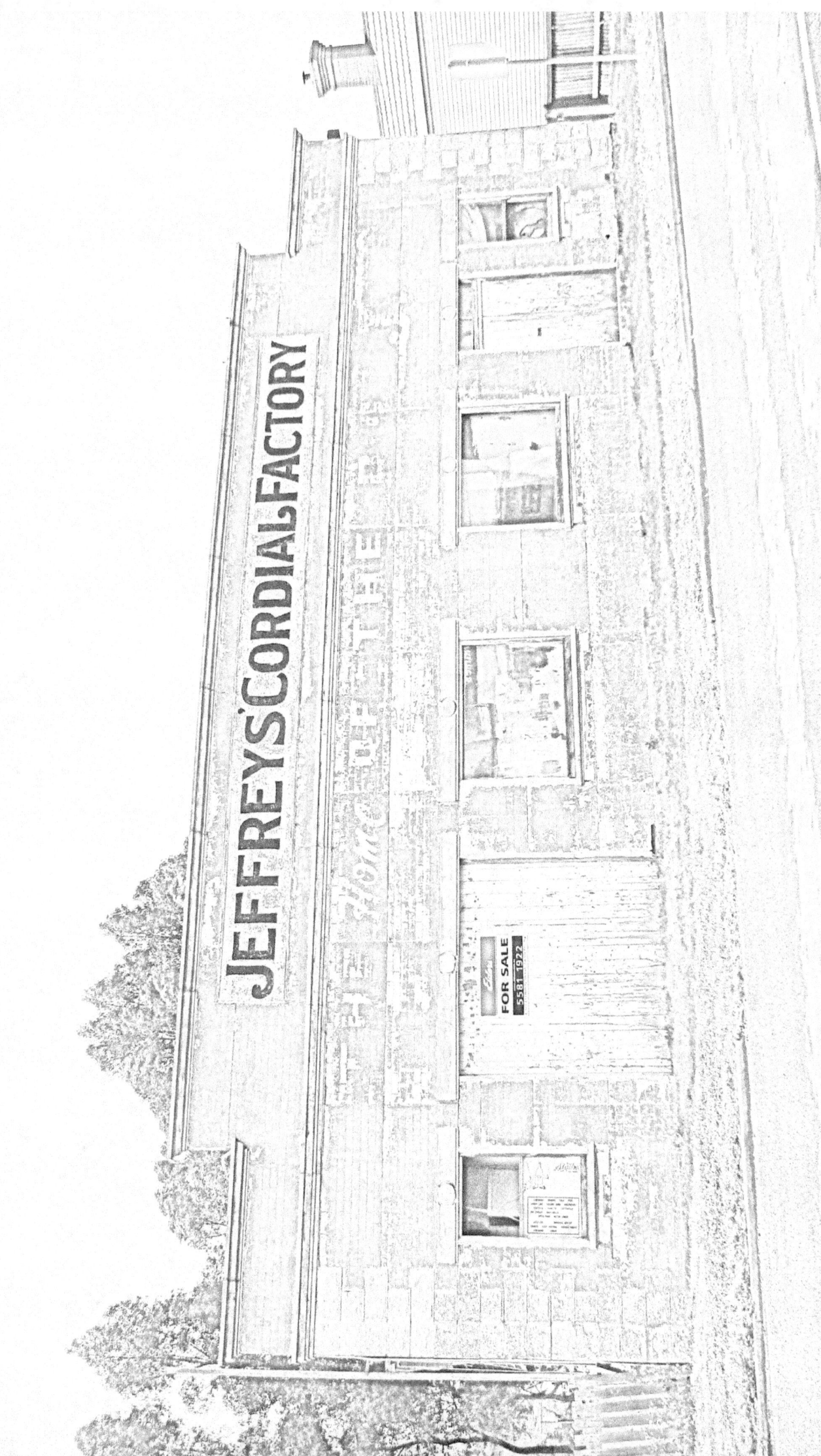

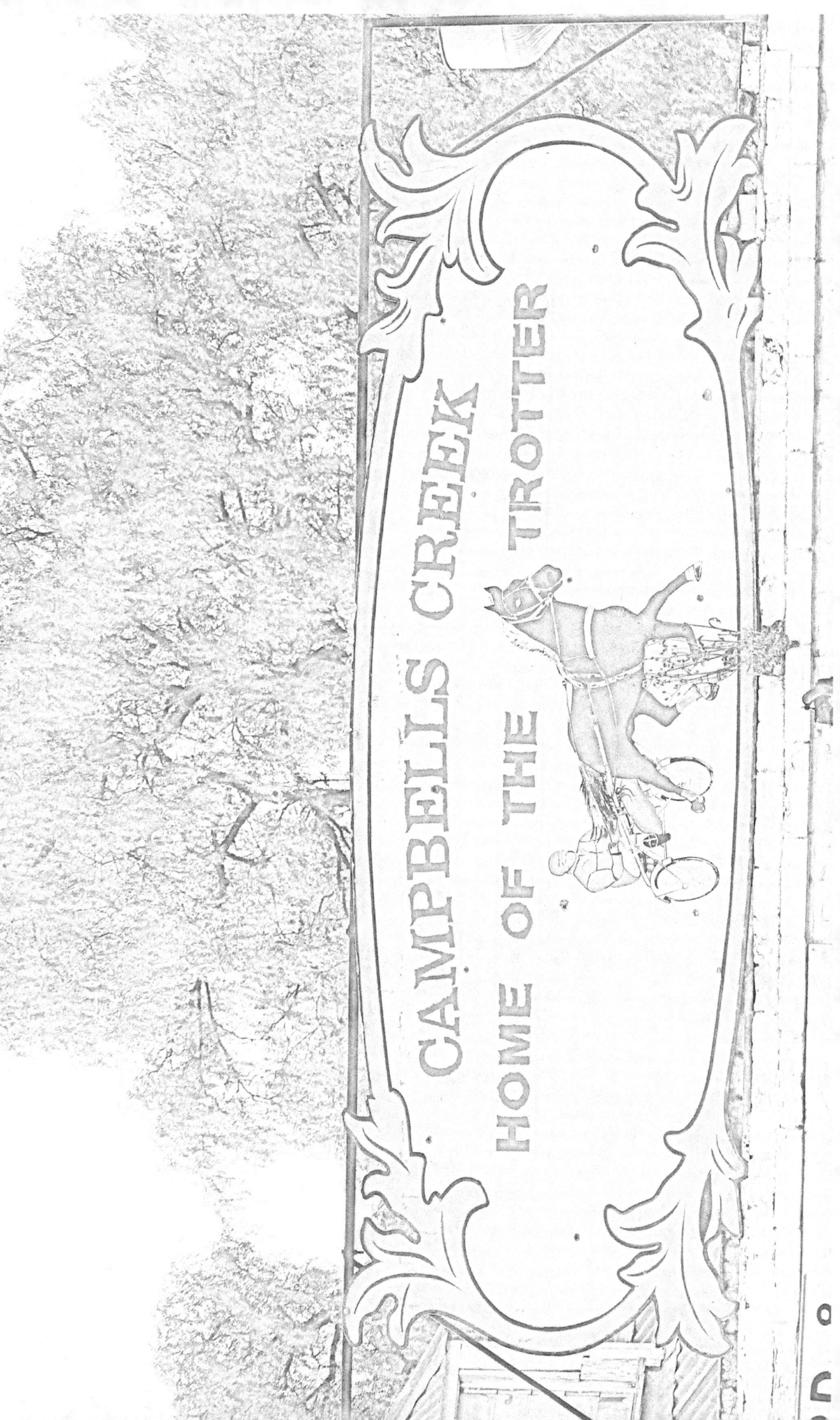

Lion

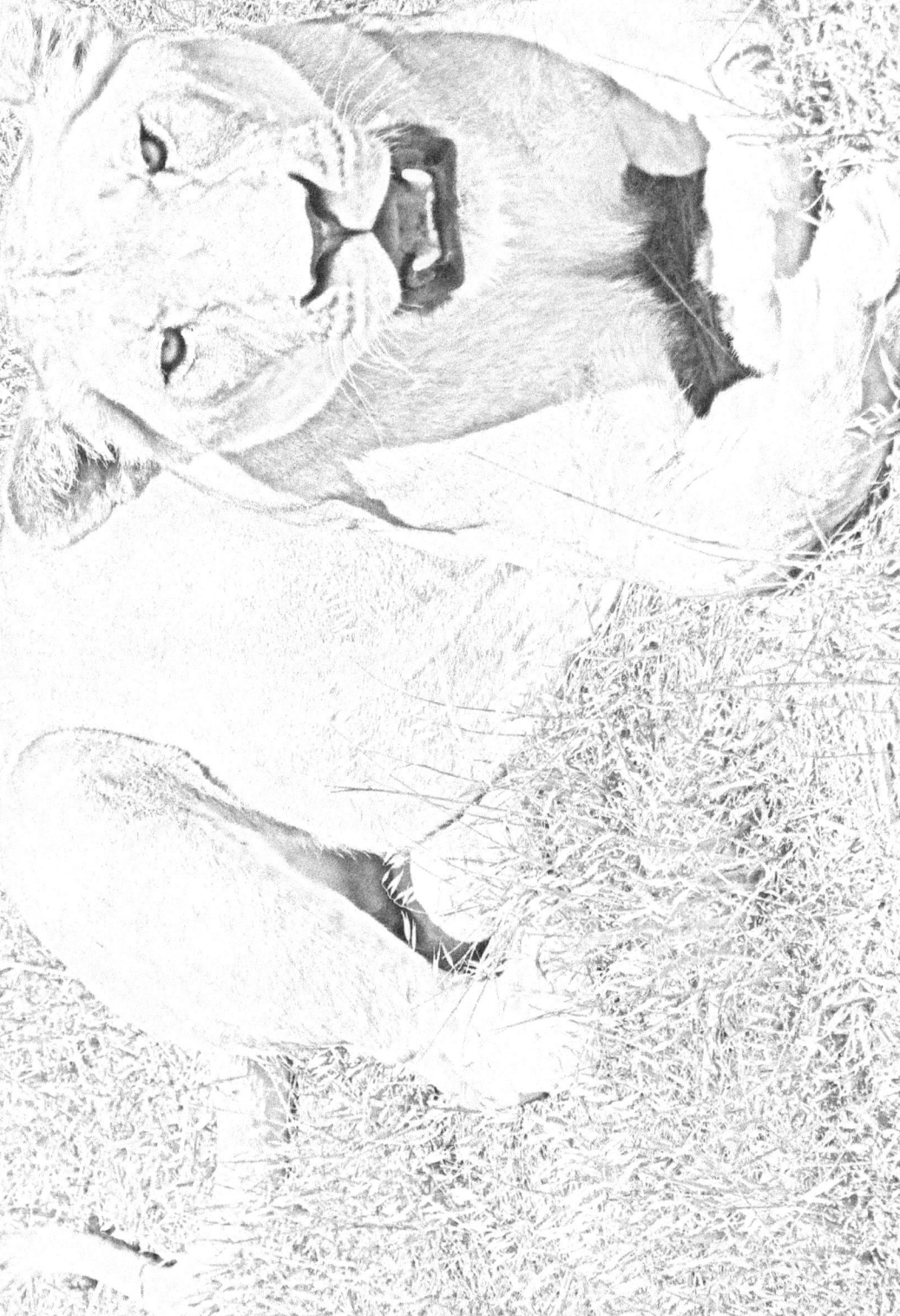

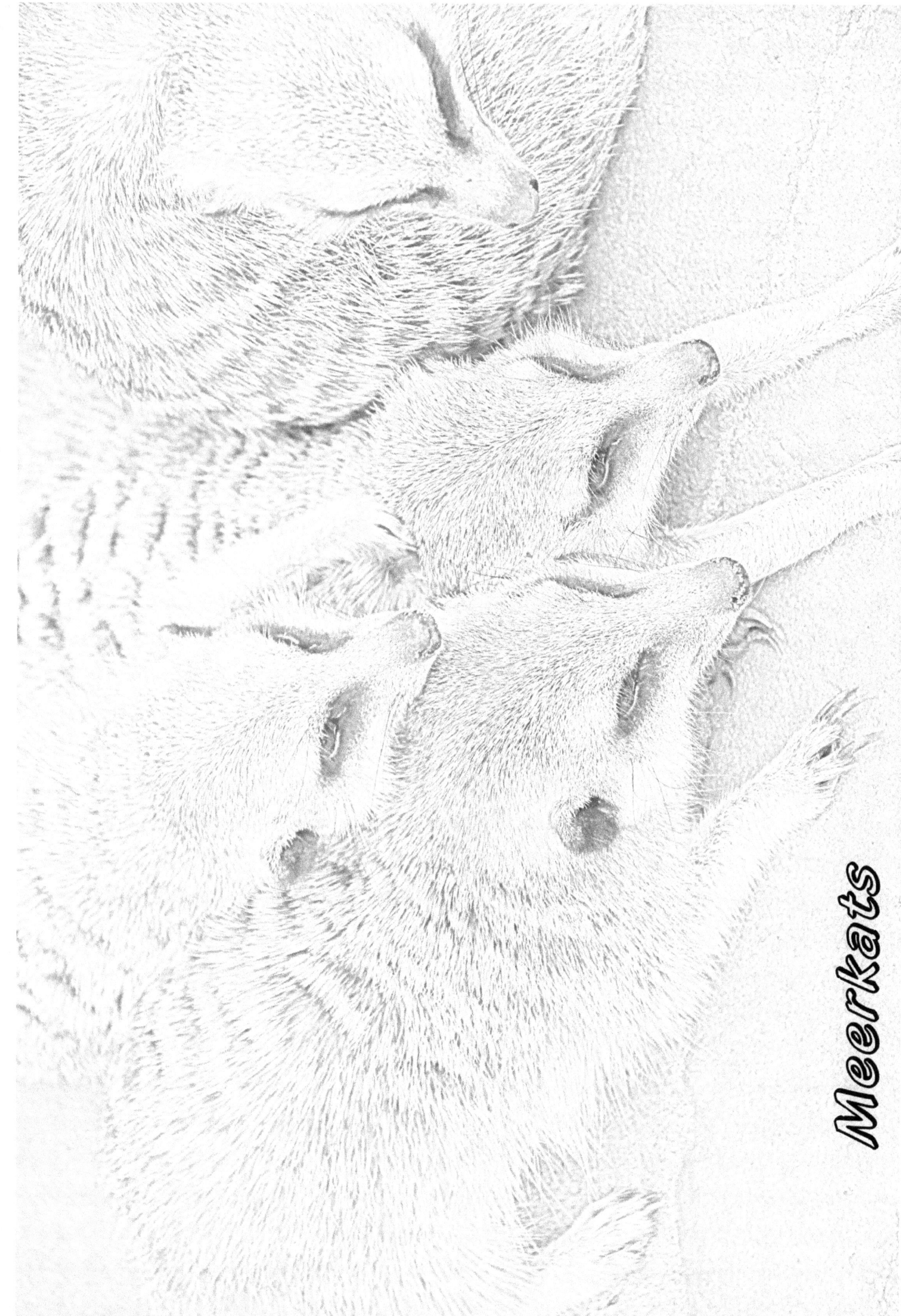

Meerkats

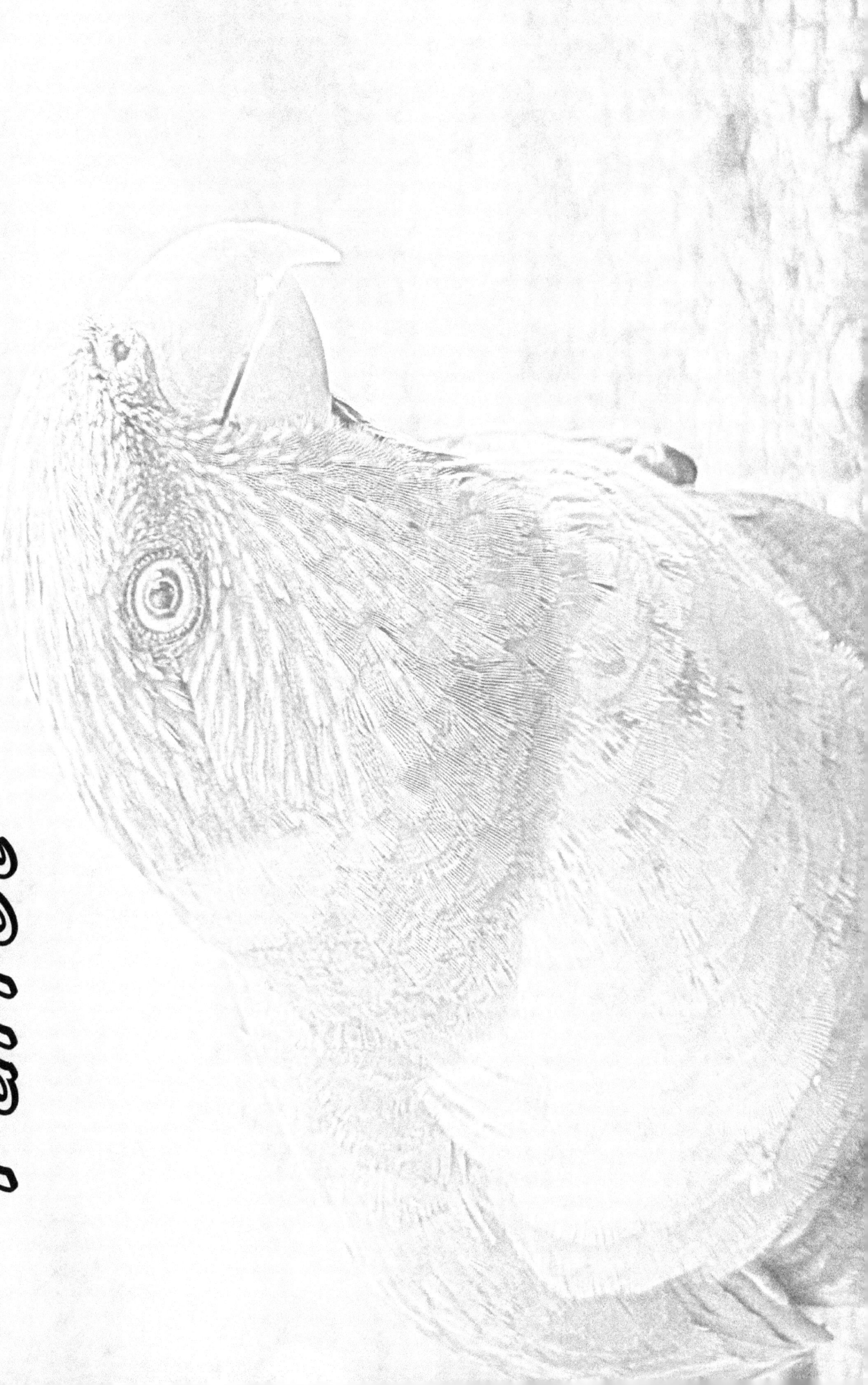

Parrot

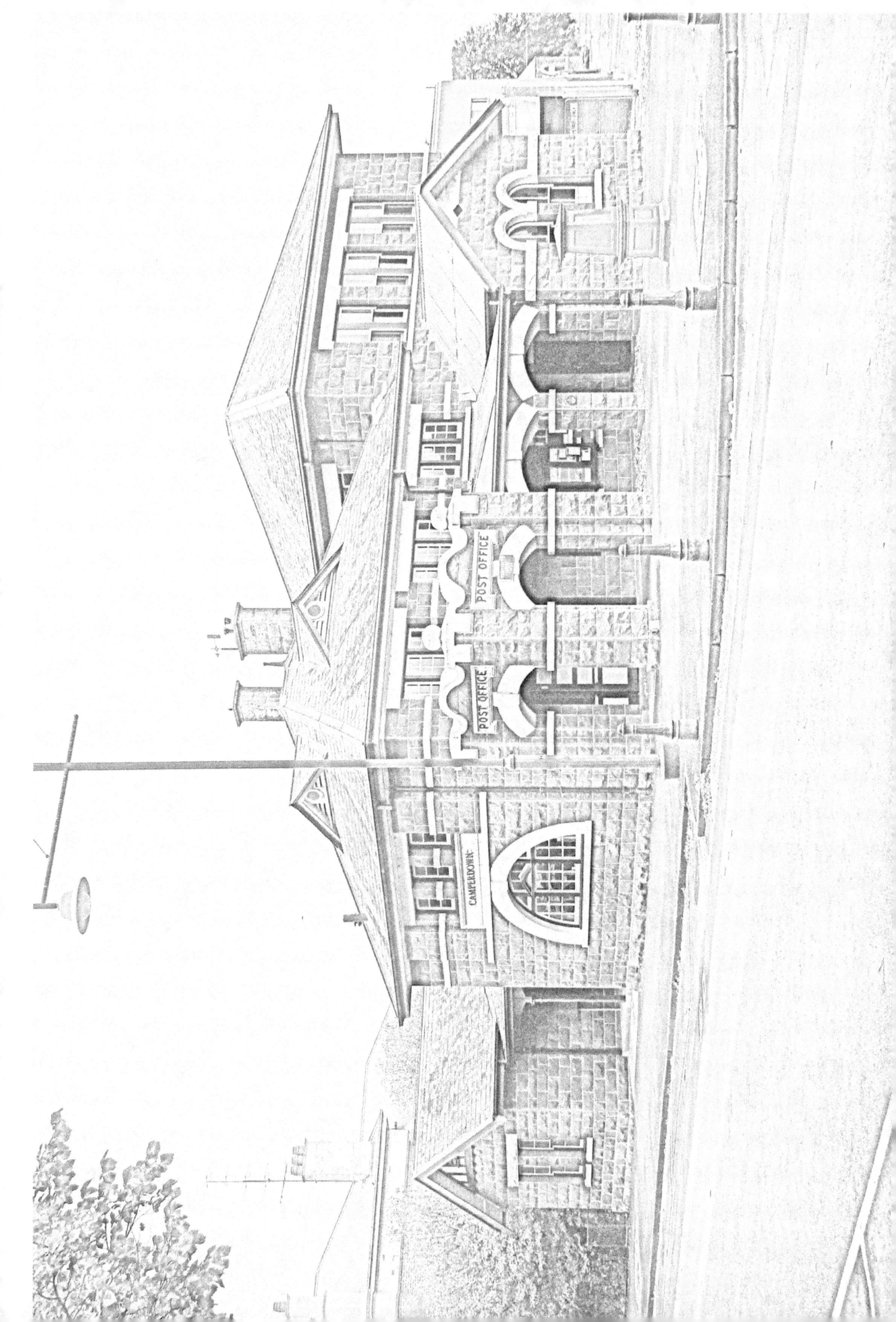

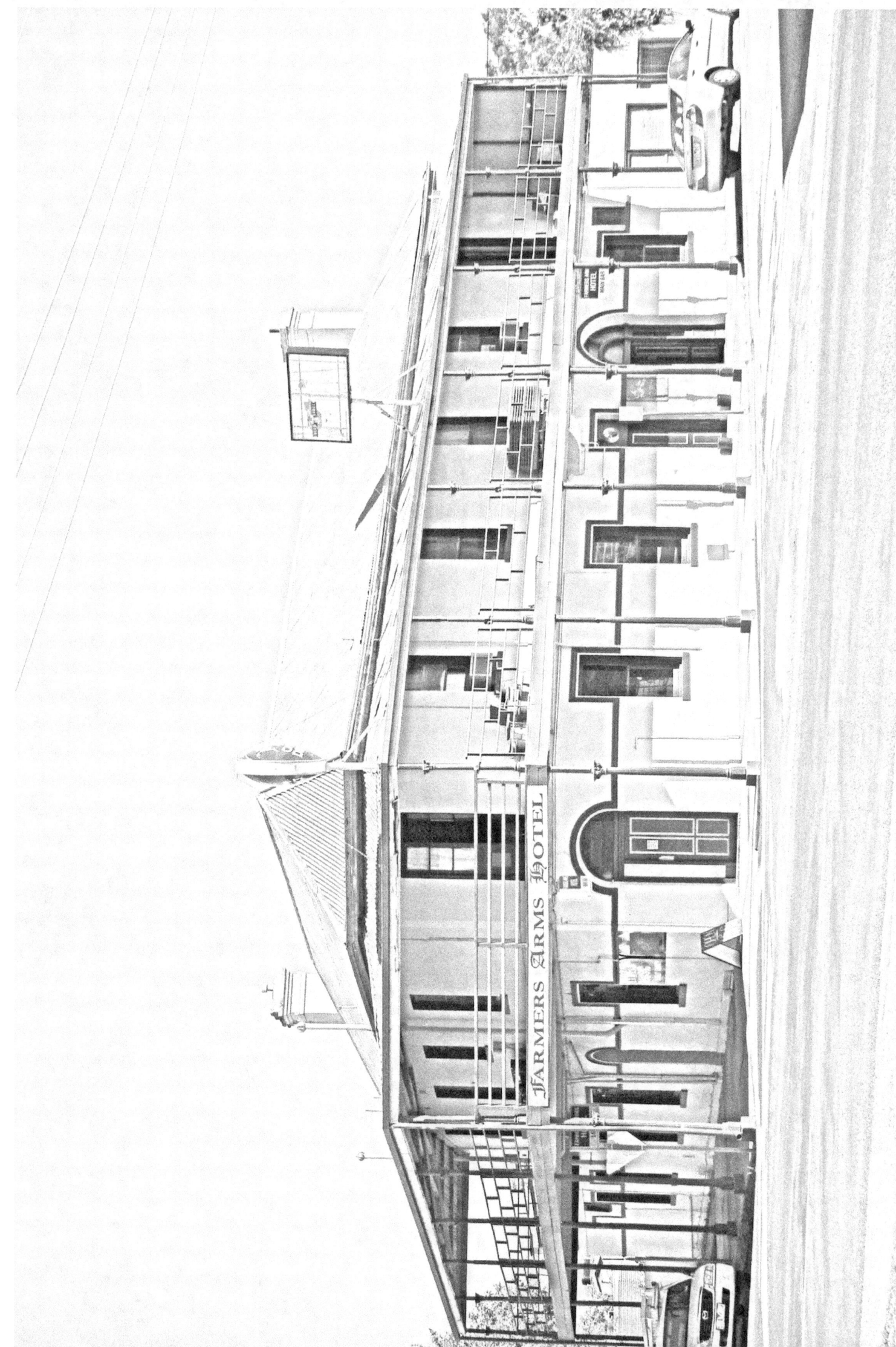

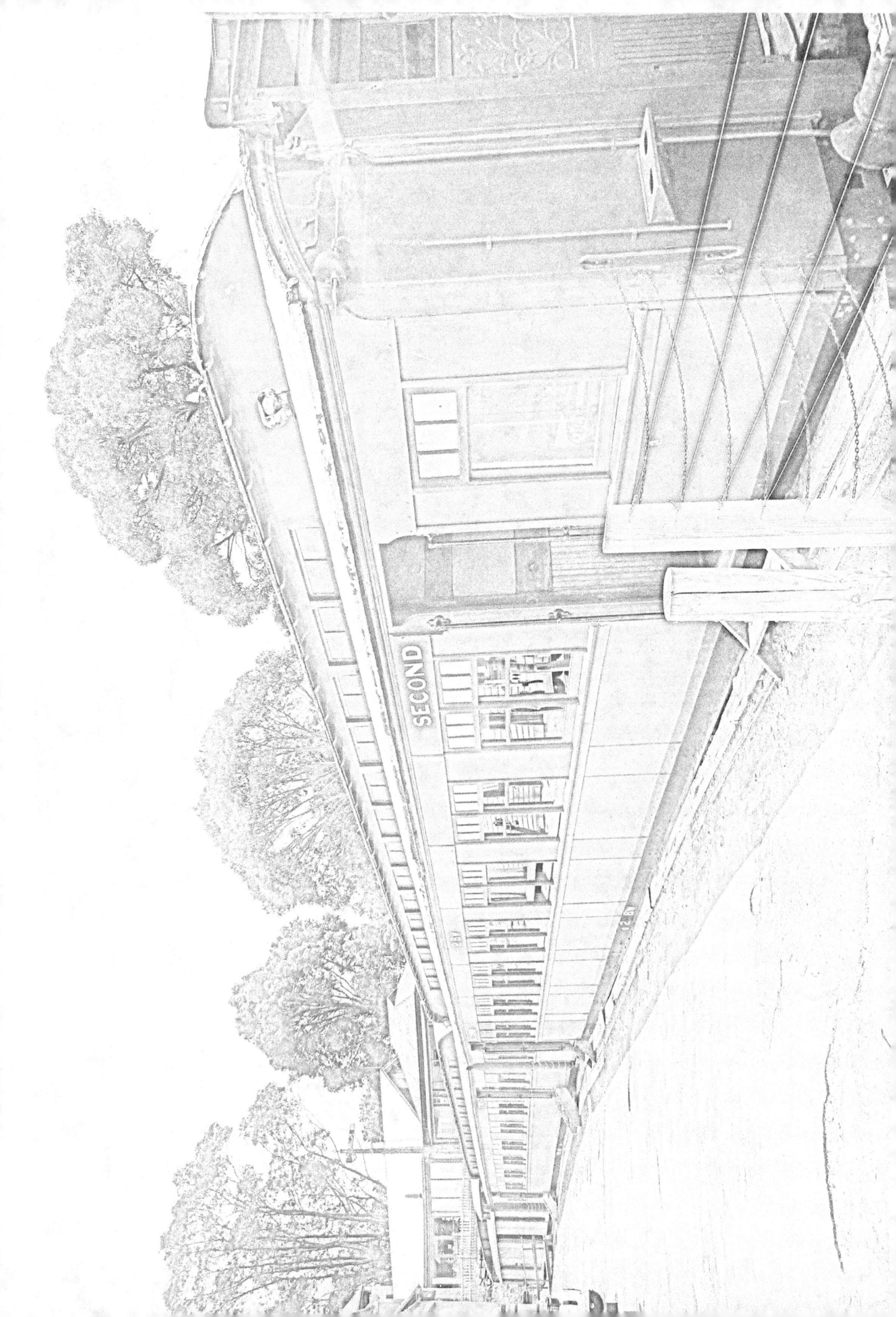

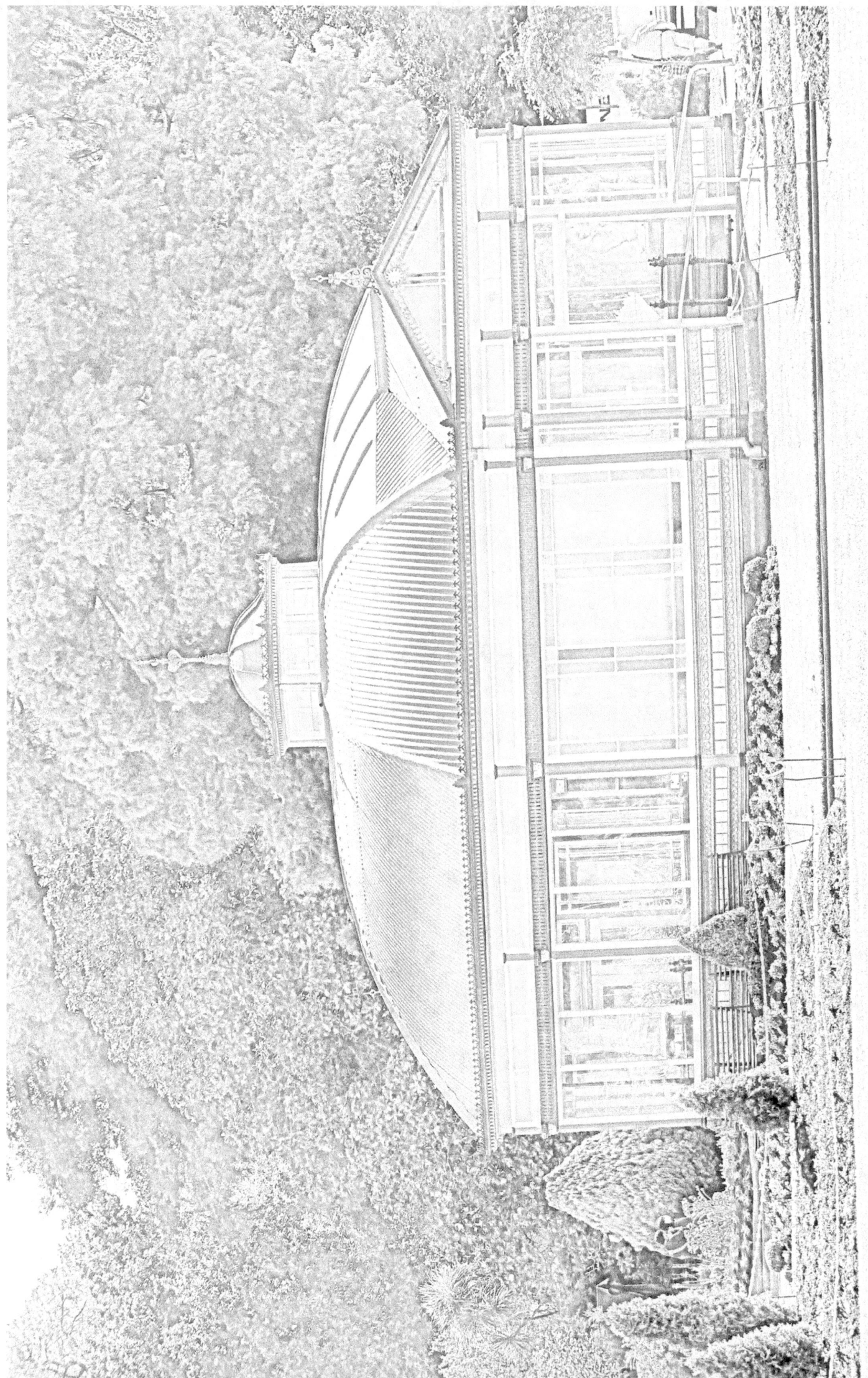

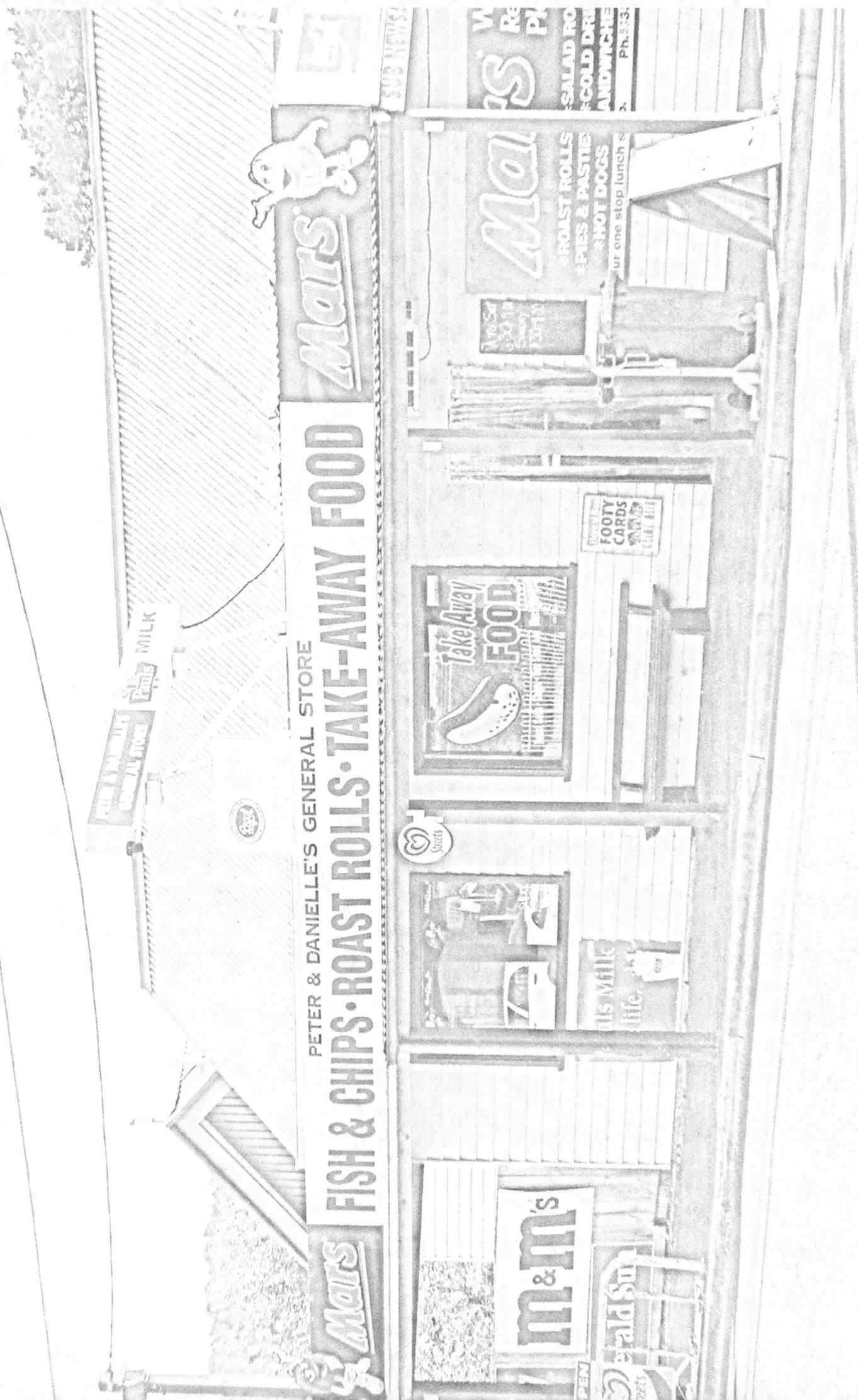

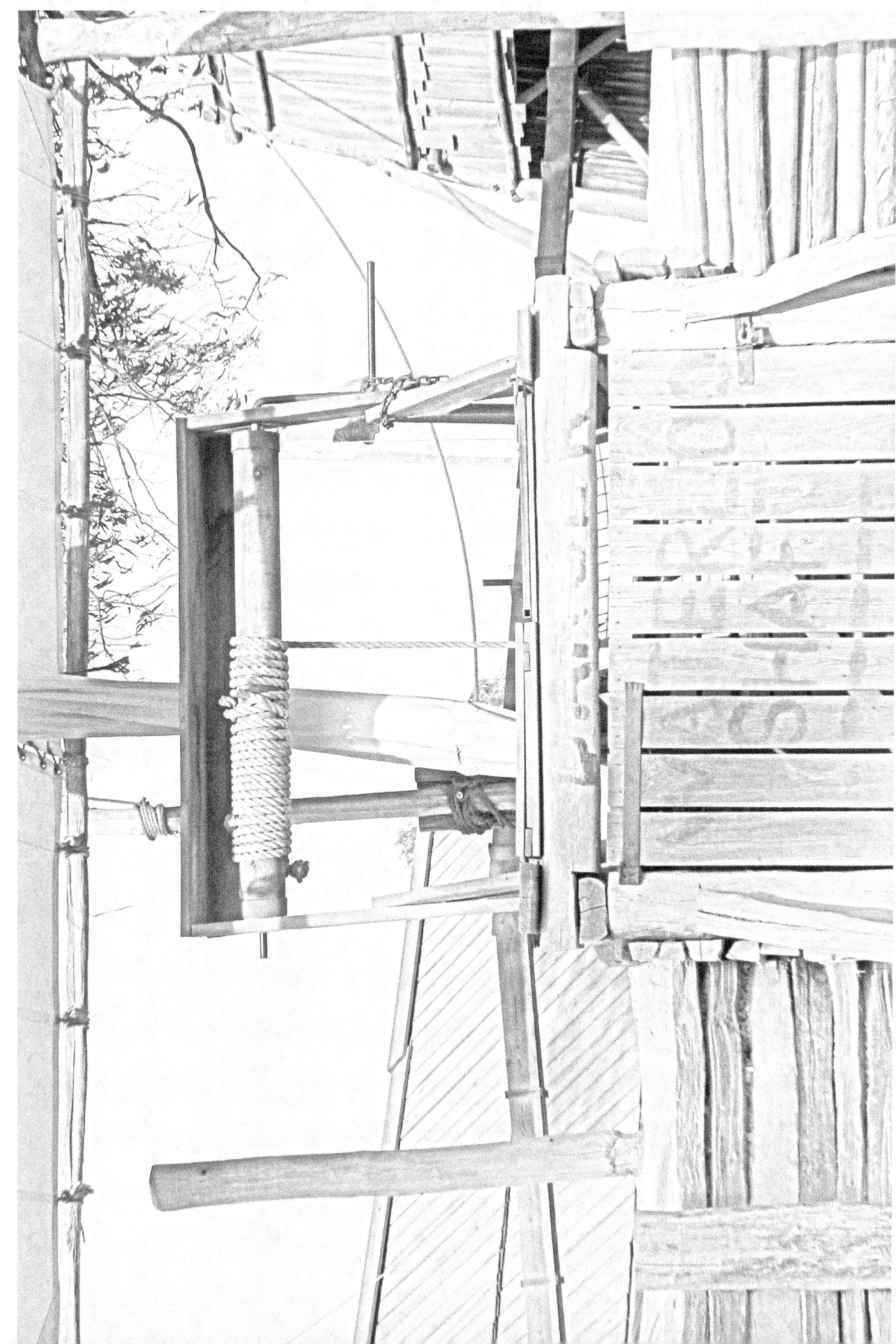

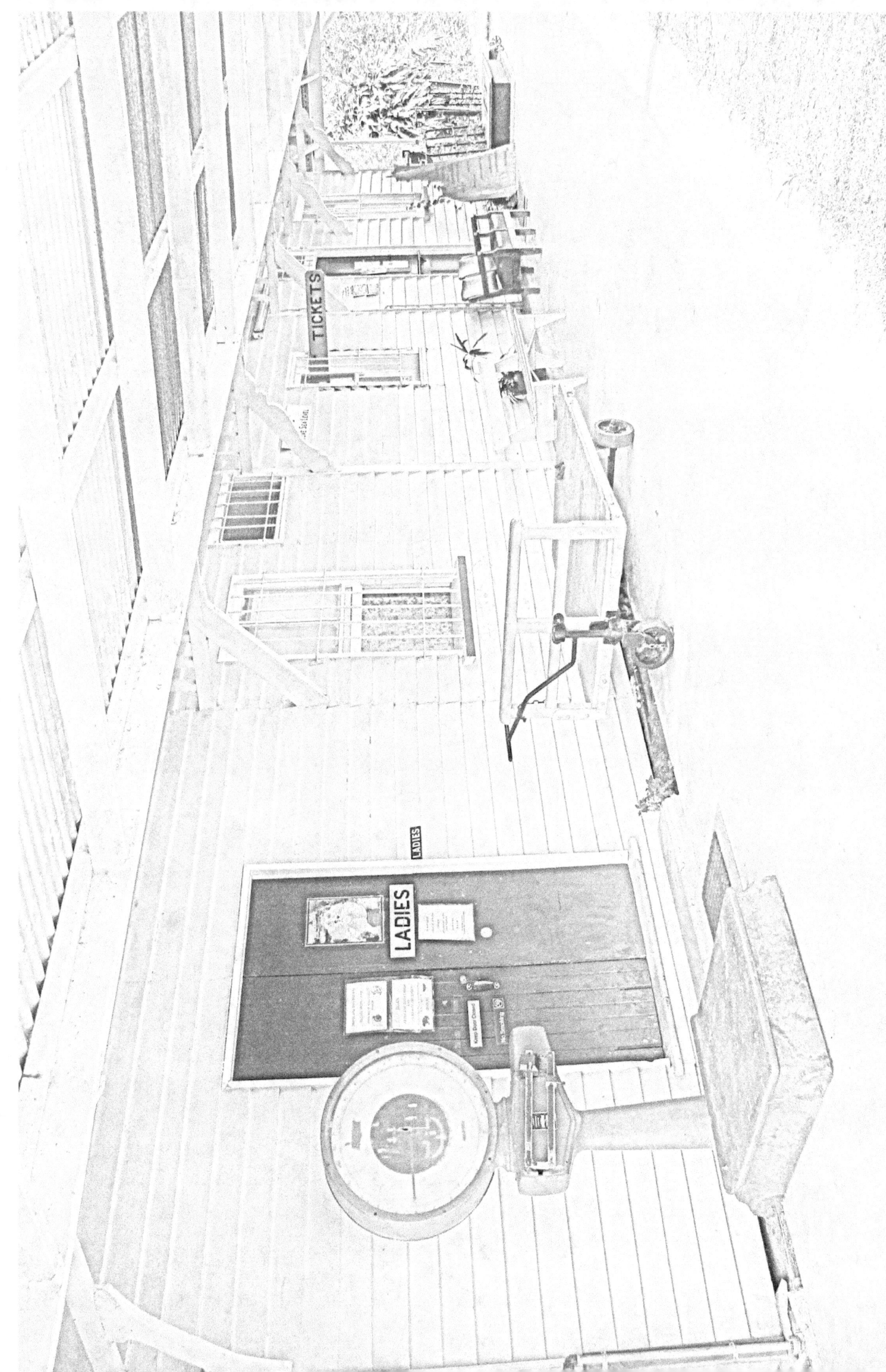

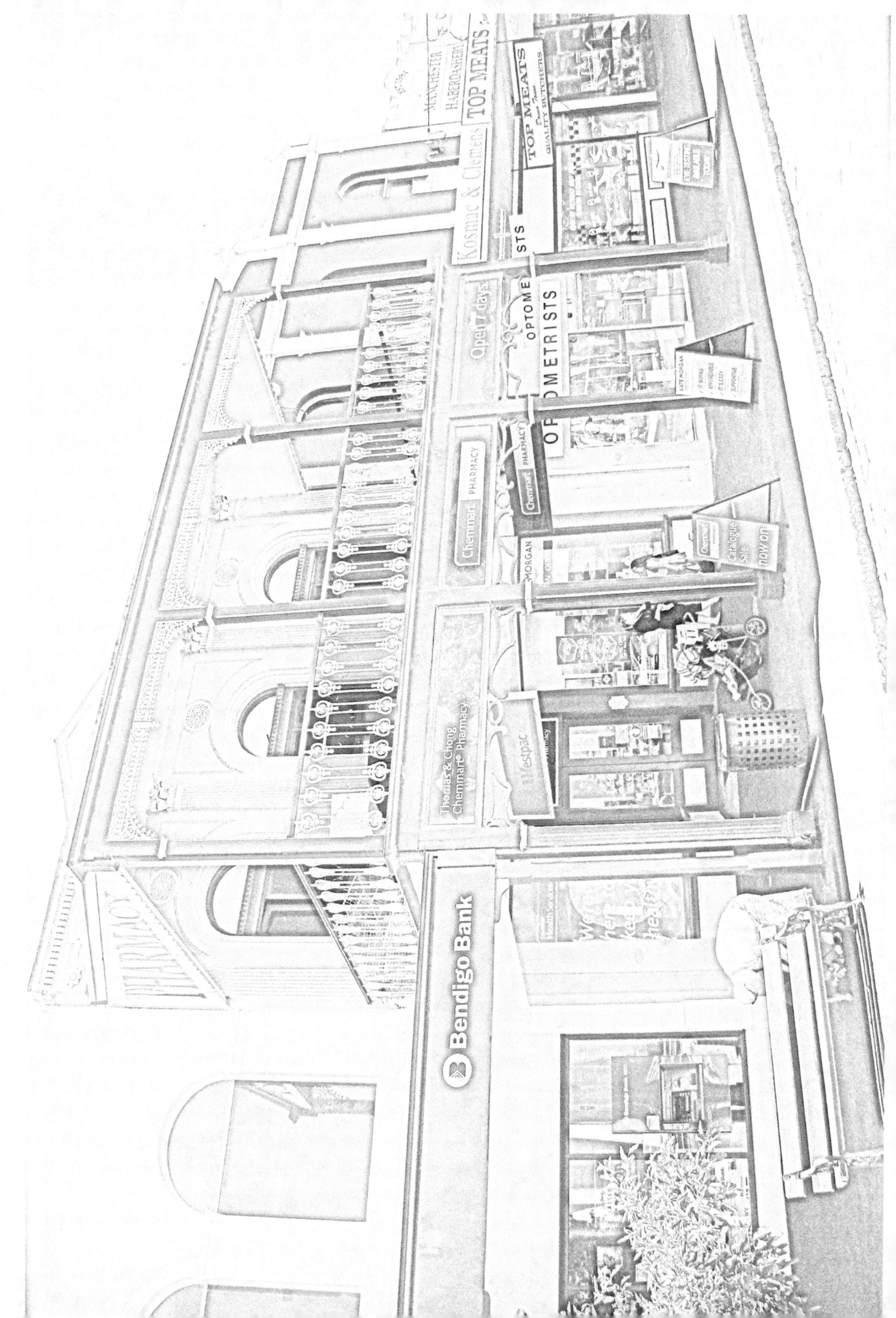

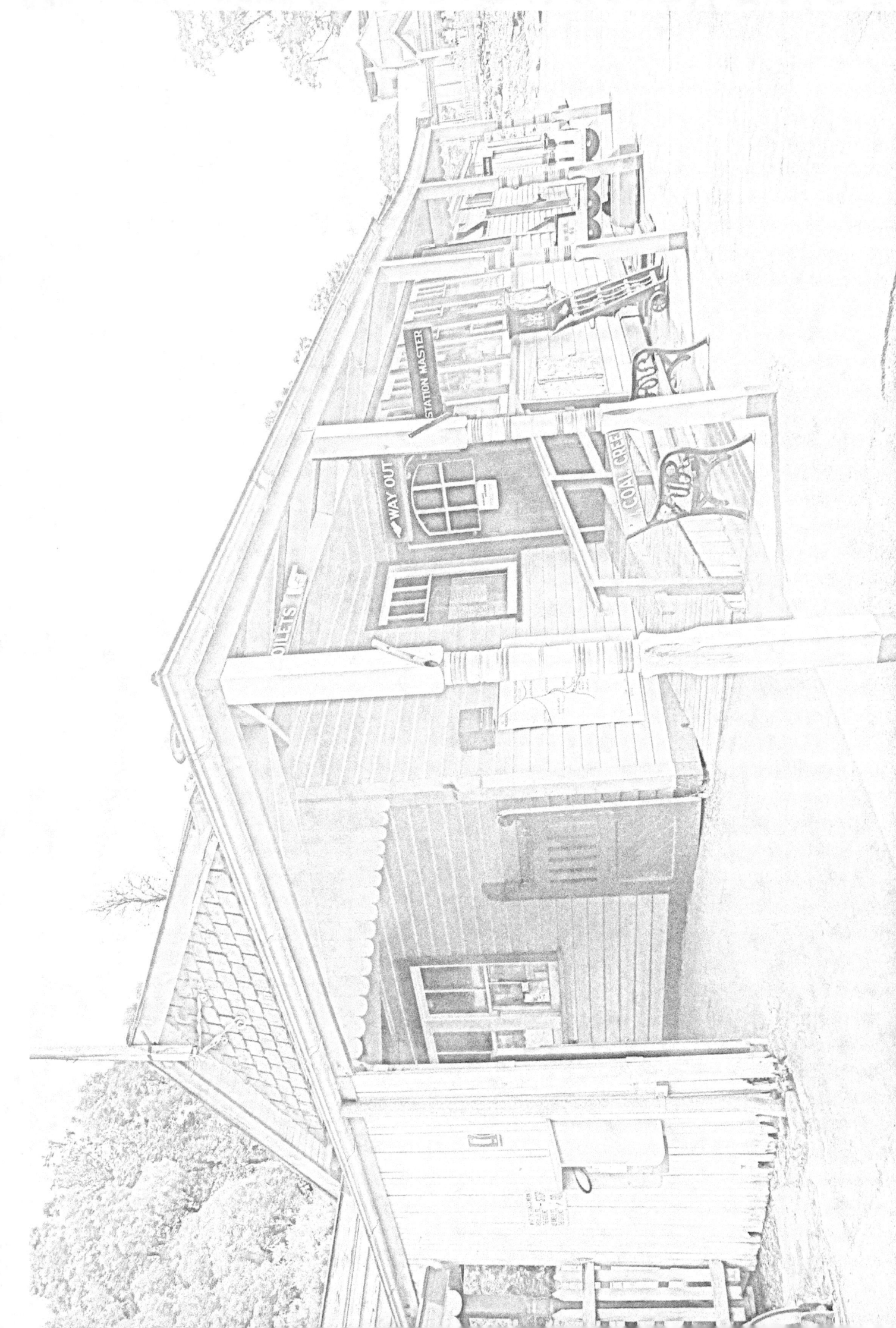

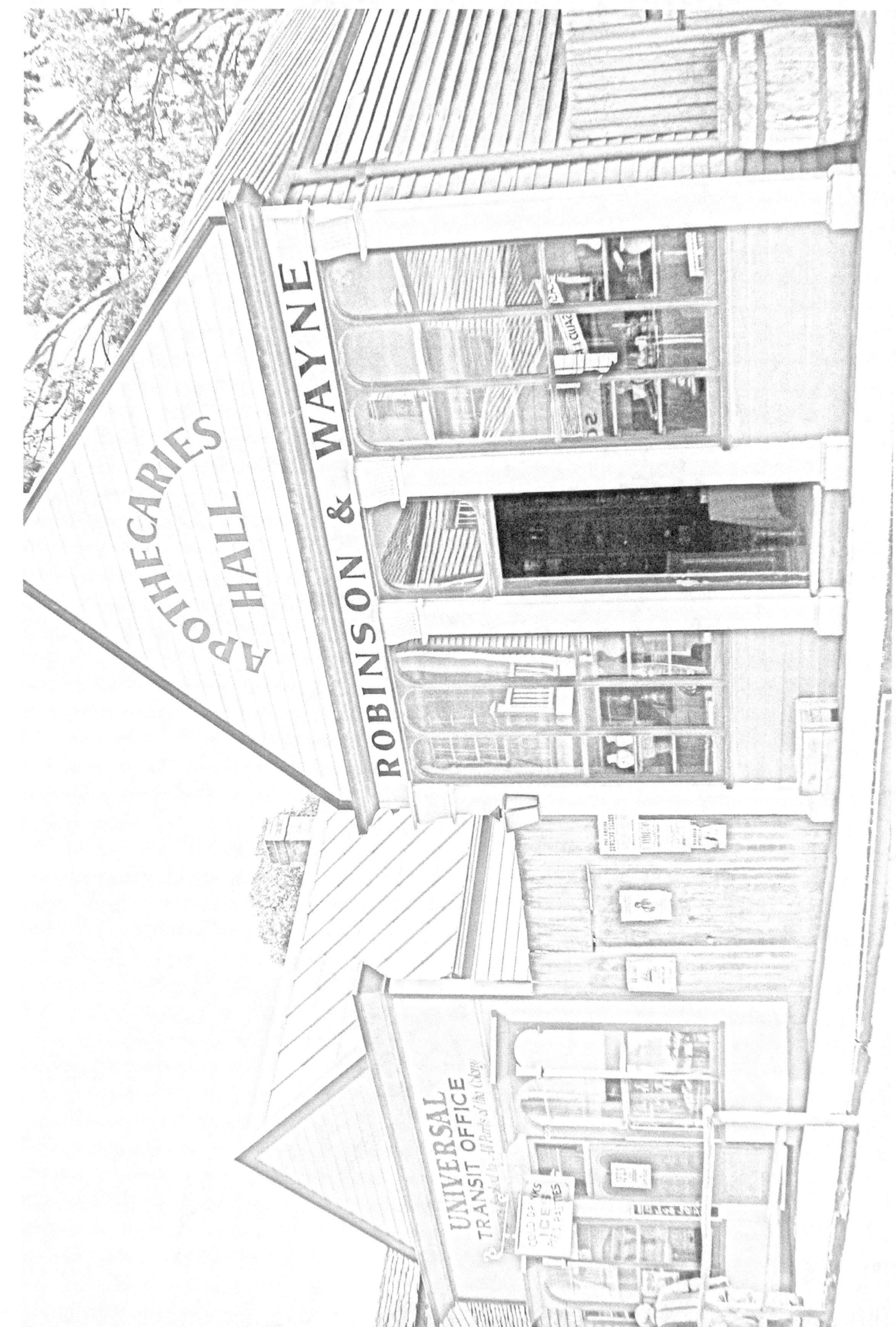

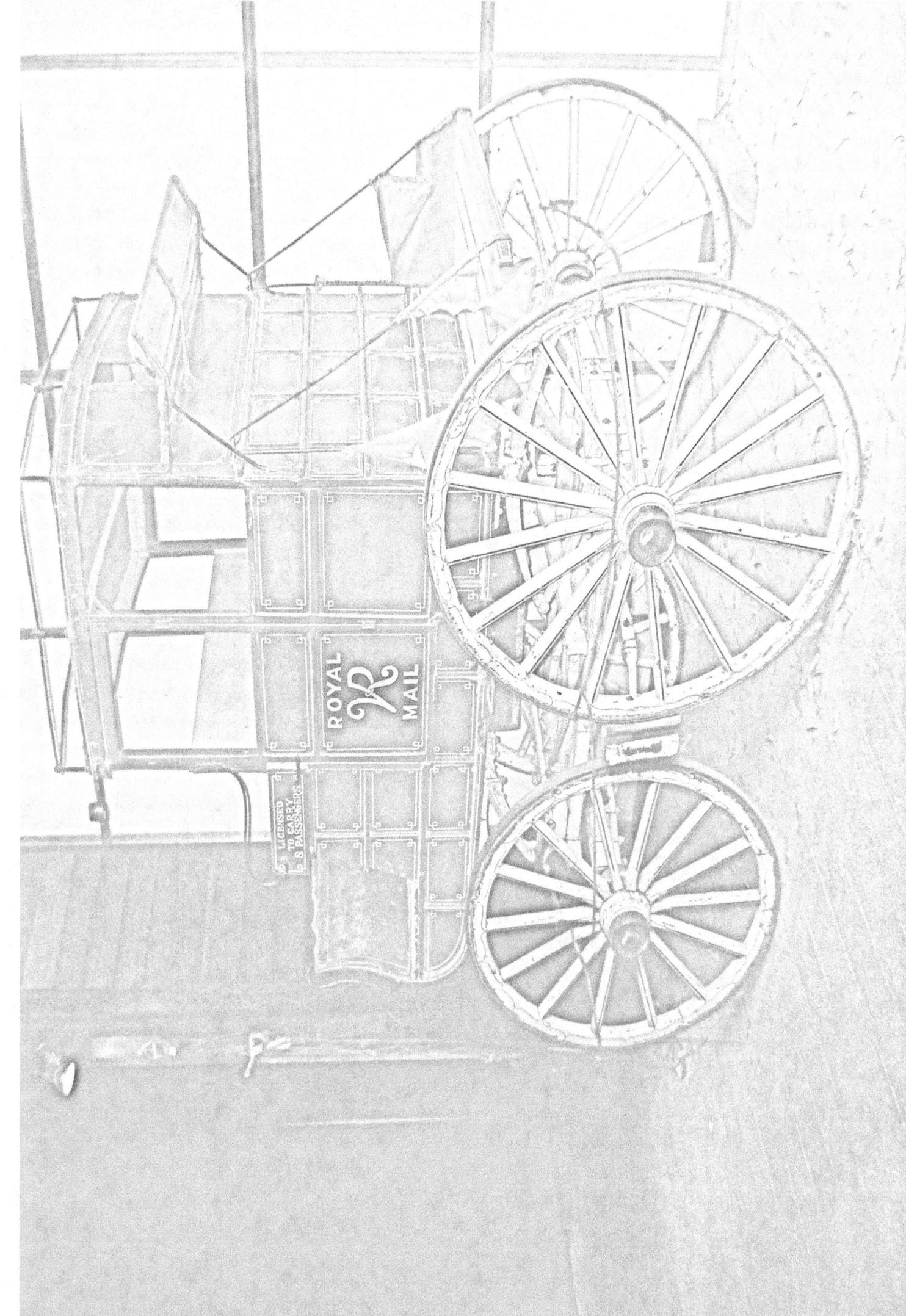

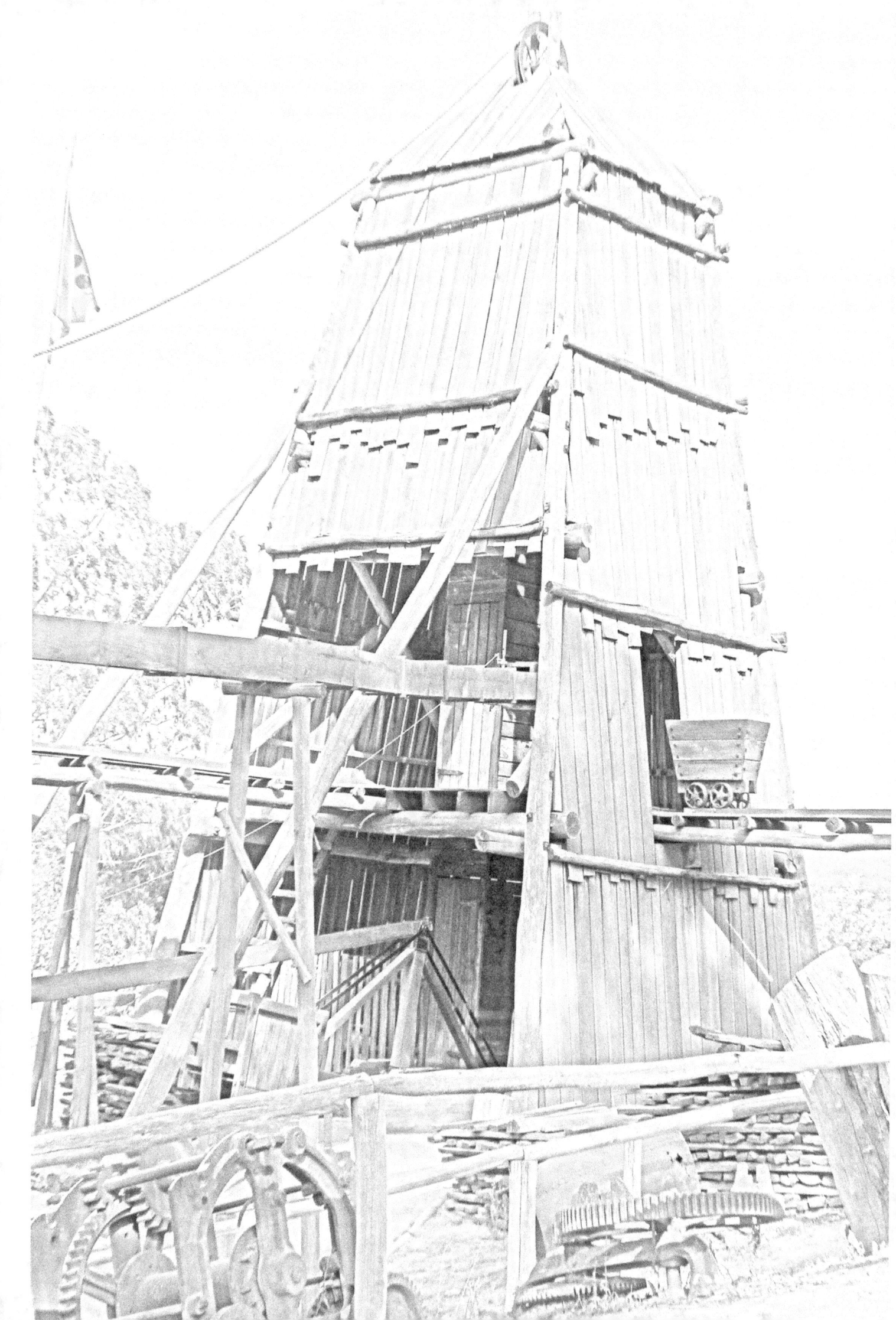

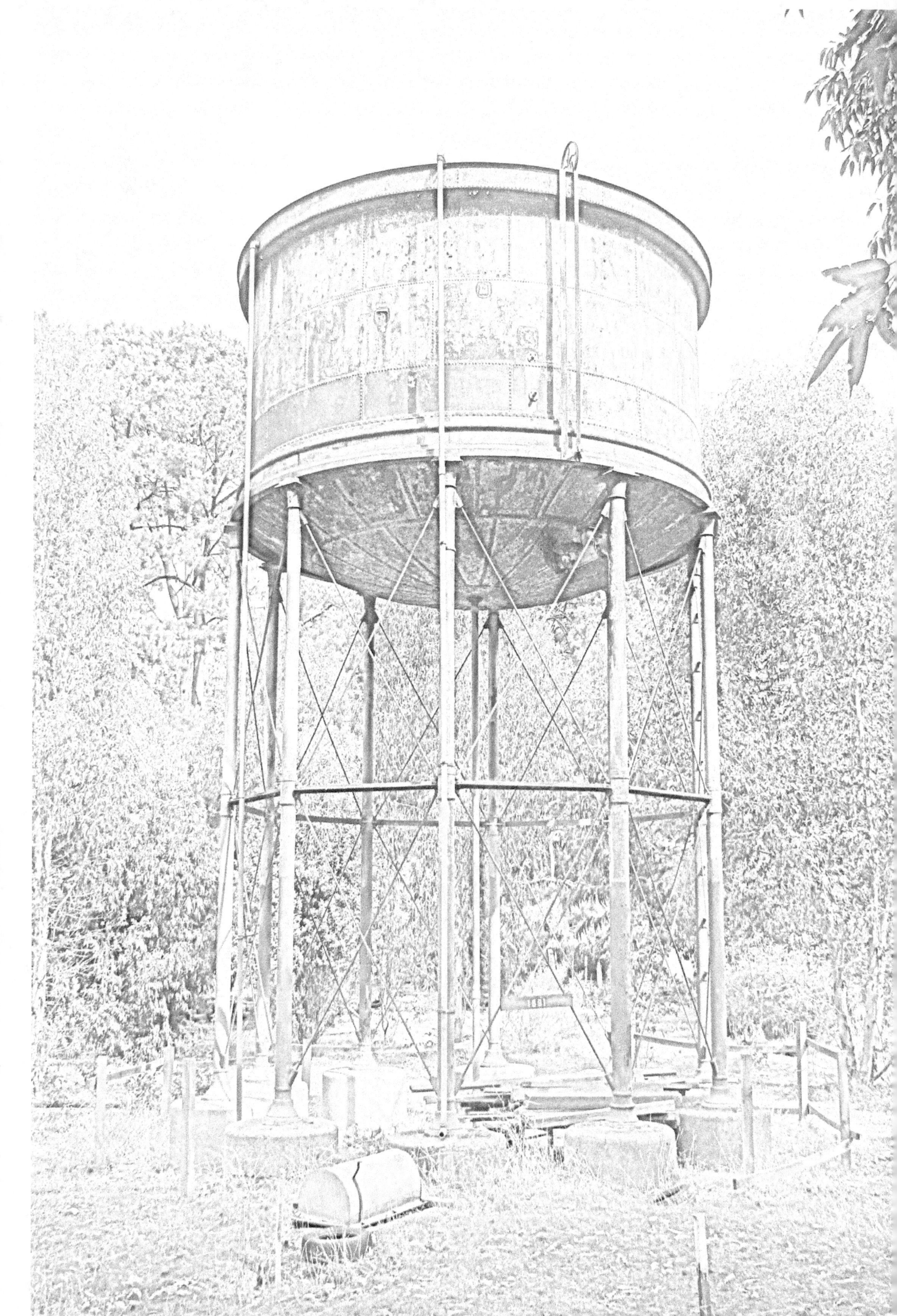

Big Truck

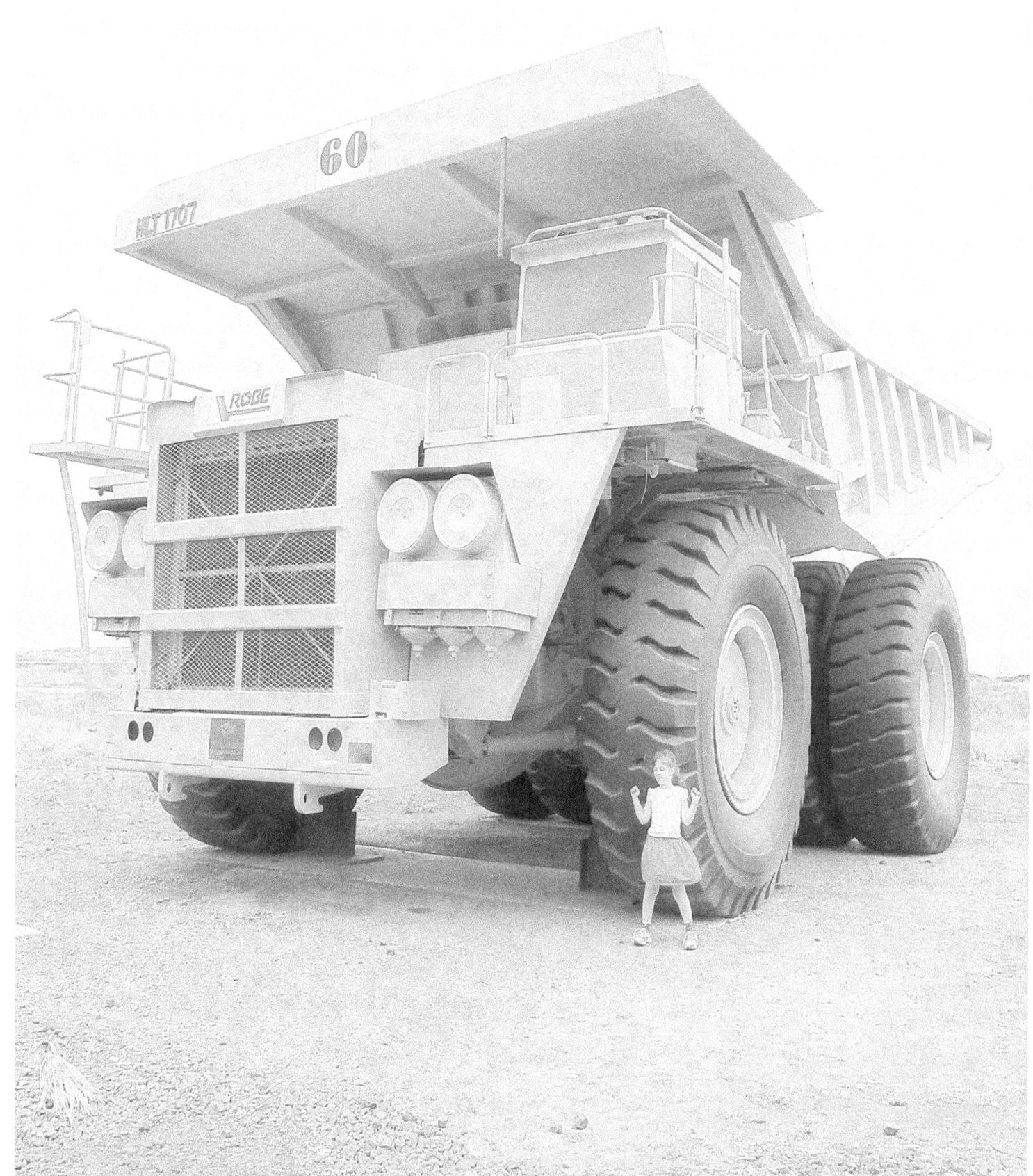

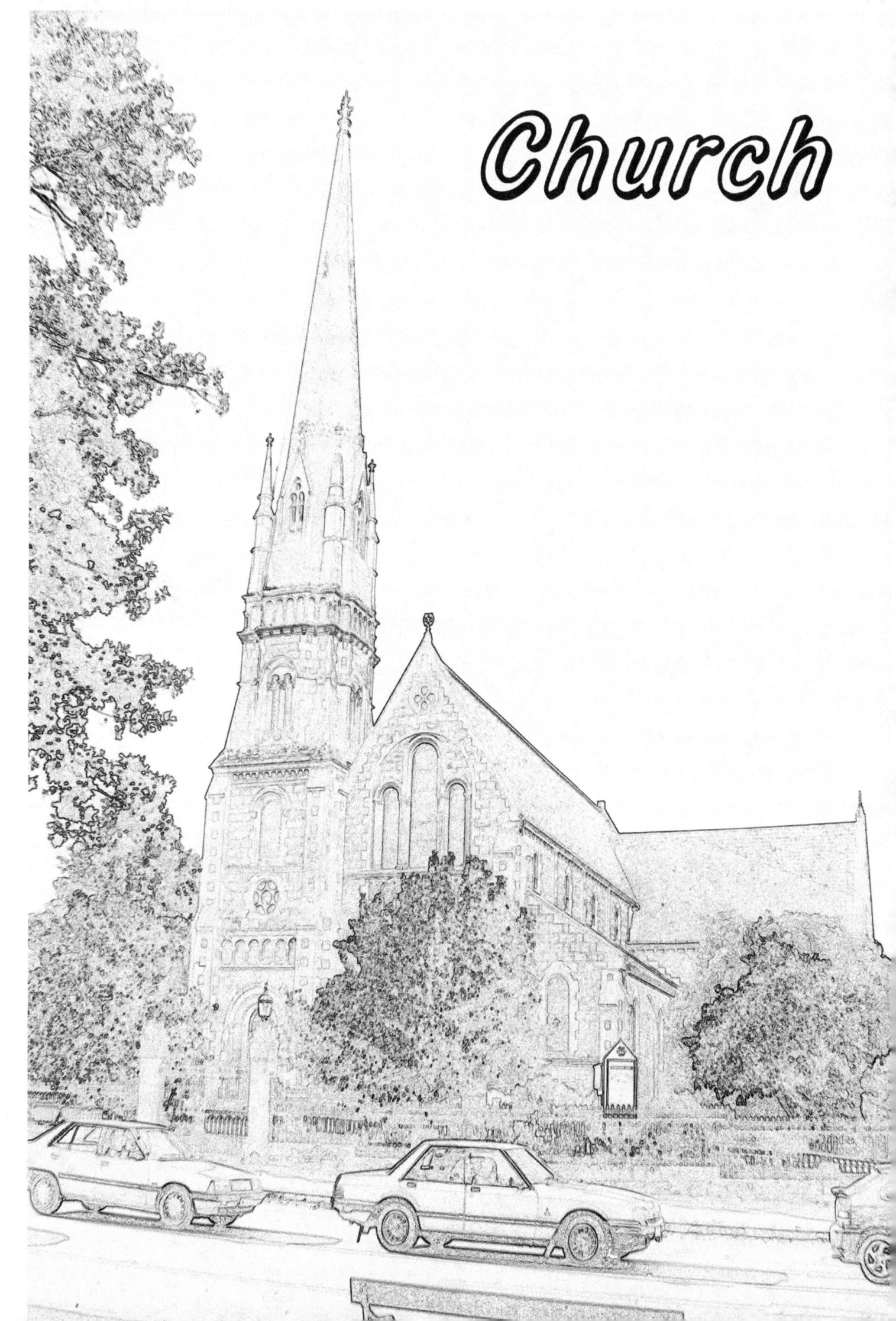

Church

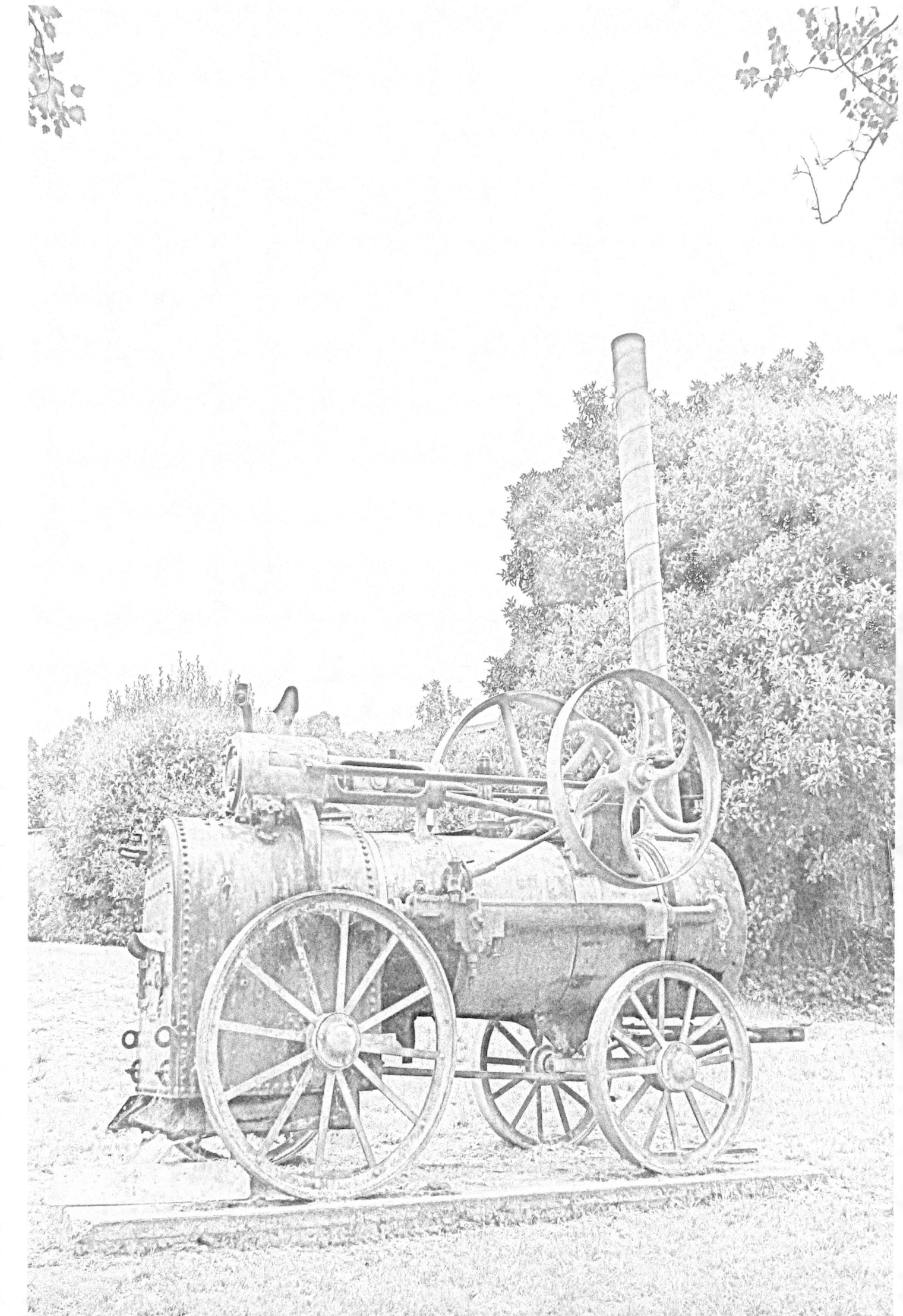

Horse

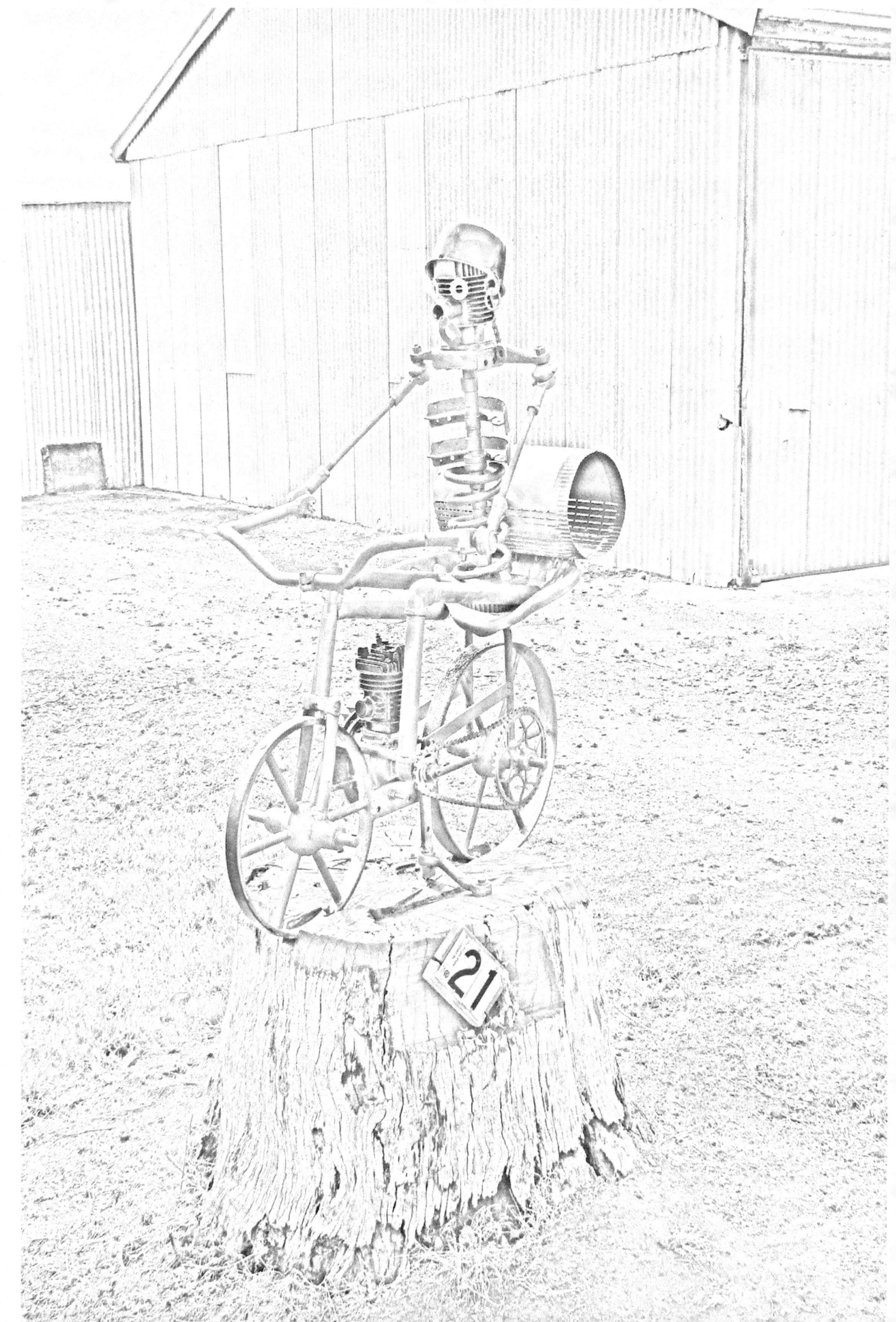

Lighthouse

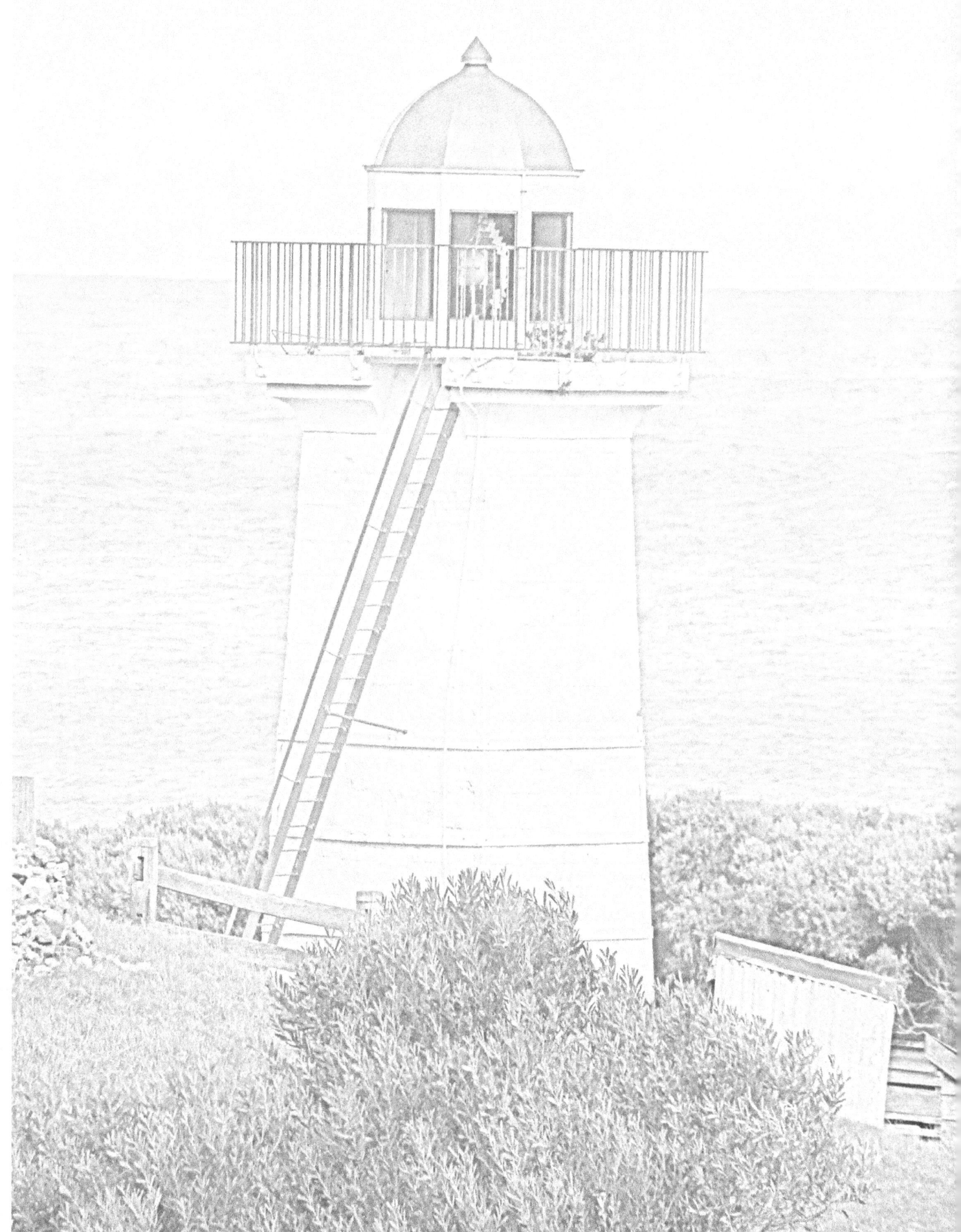

Meerkat

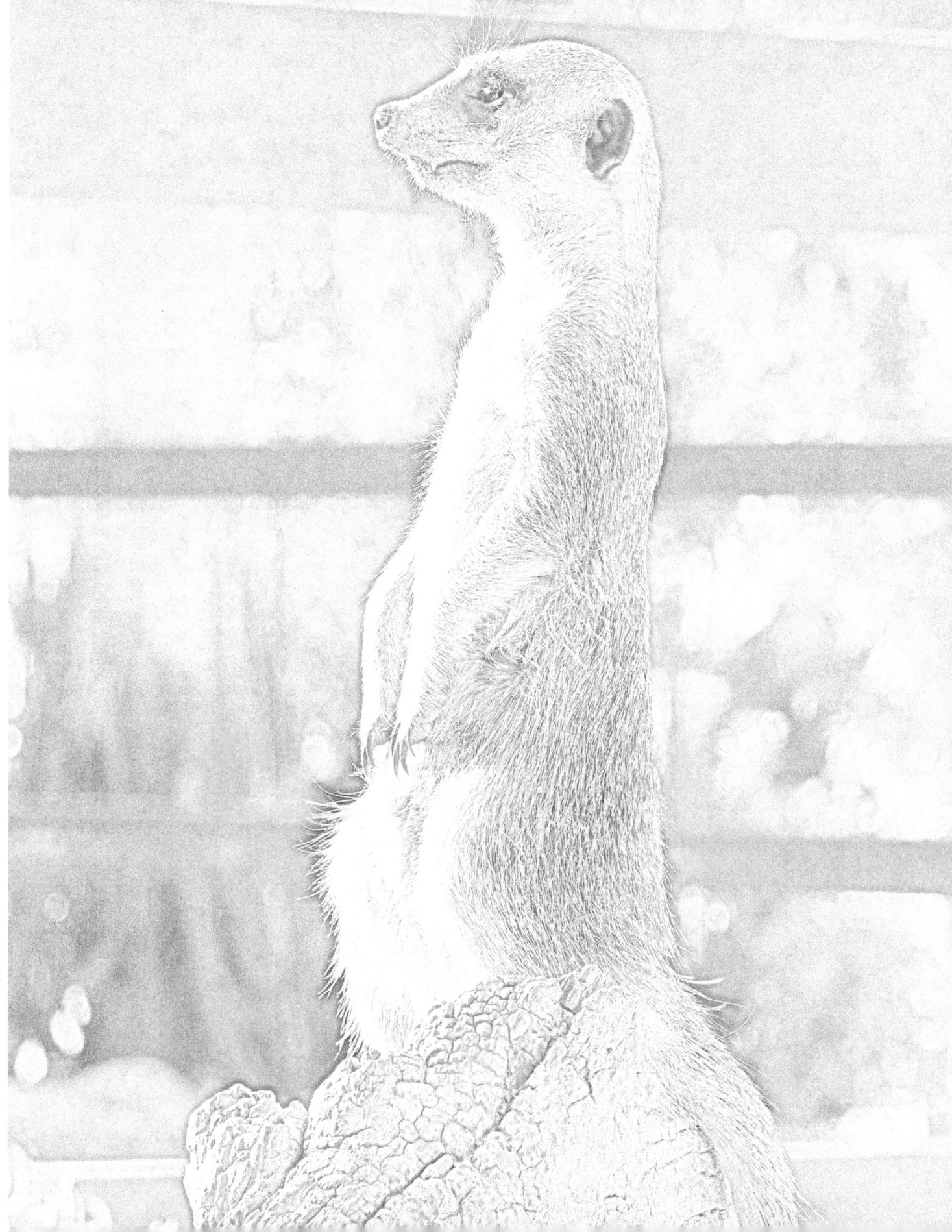

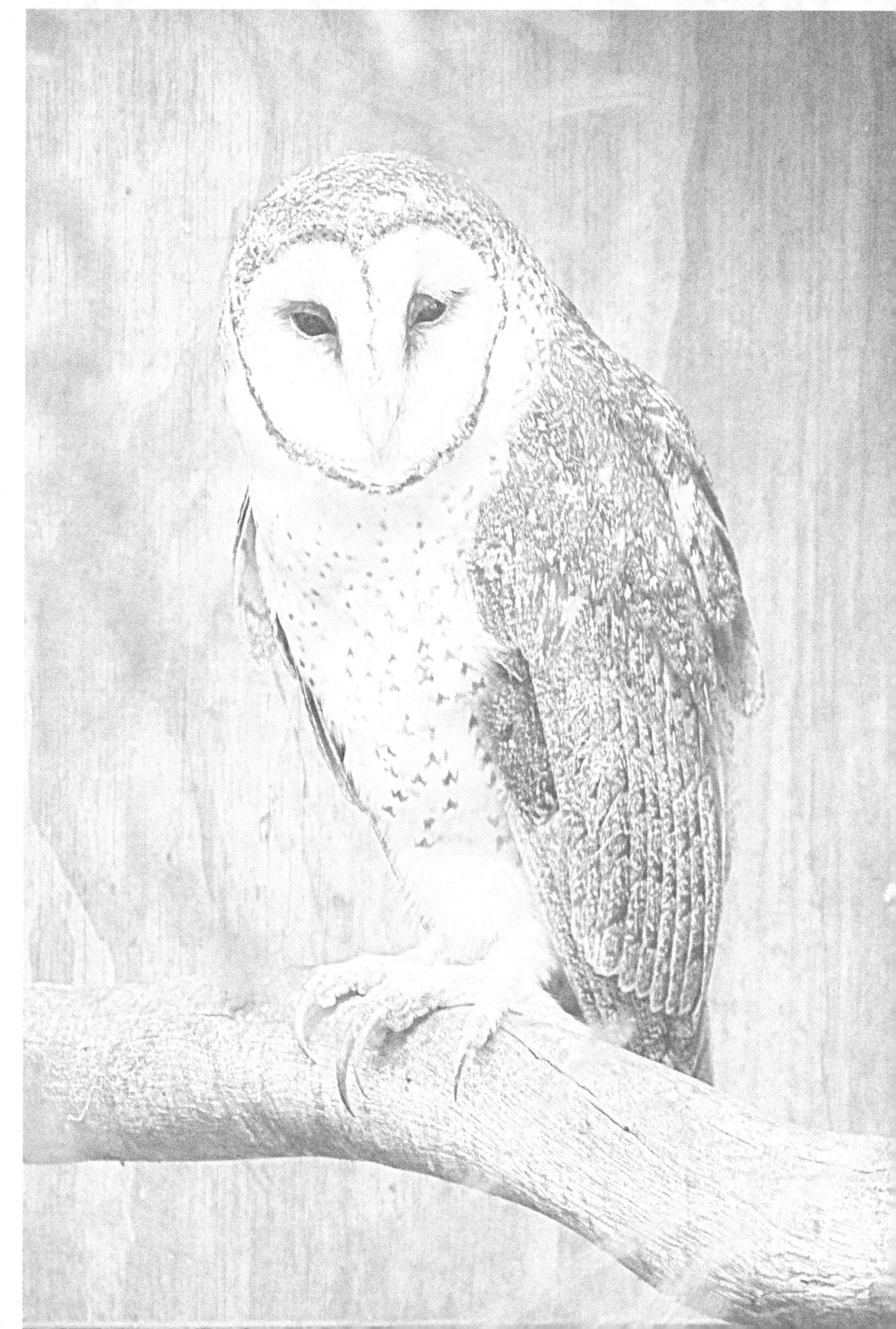

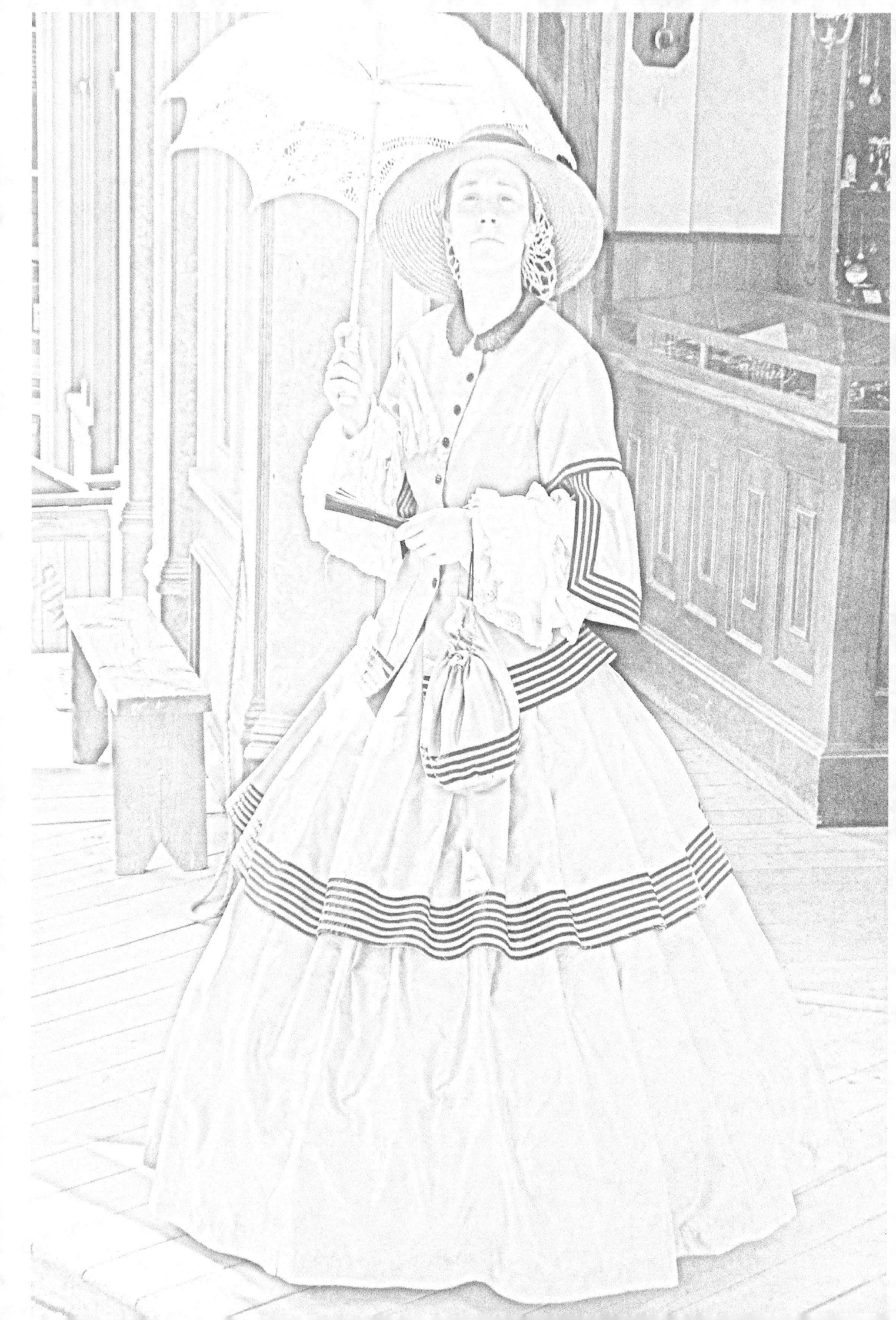

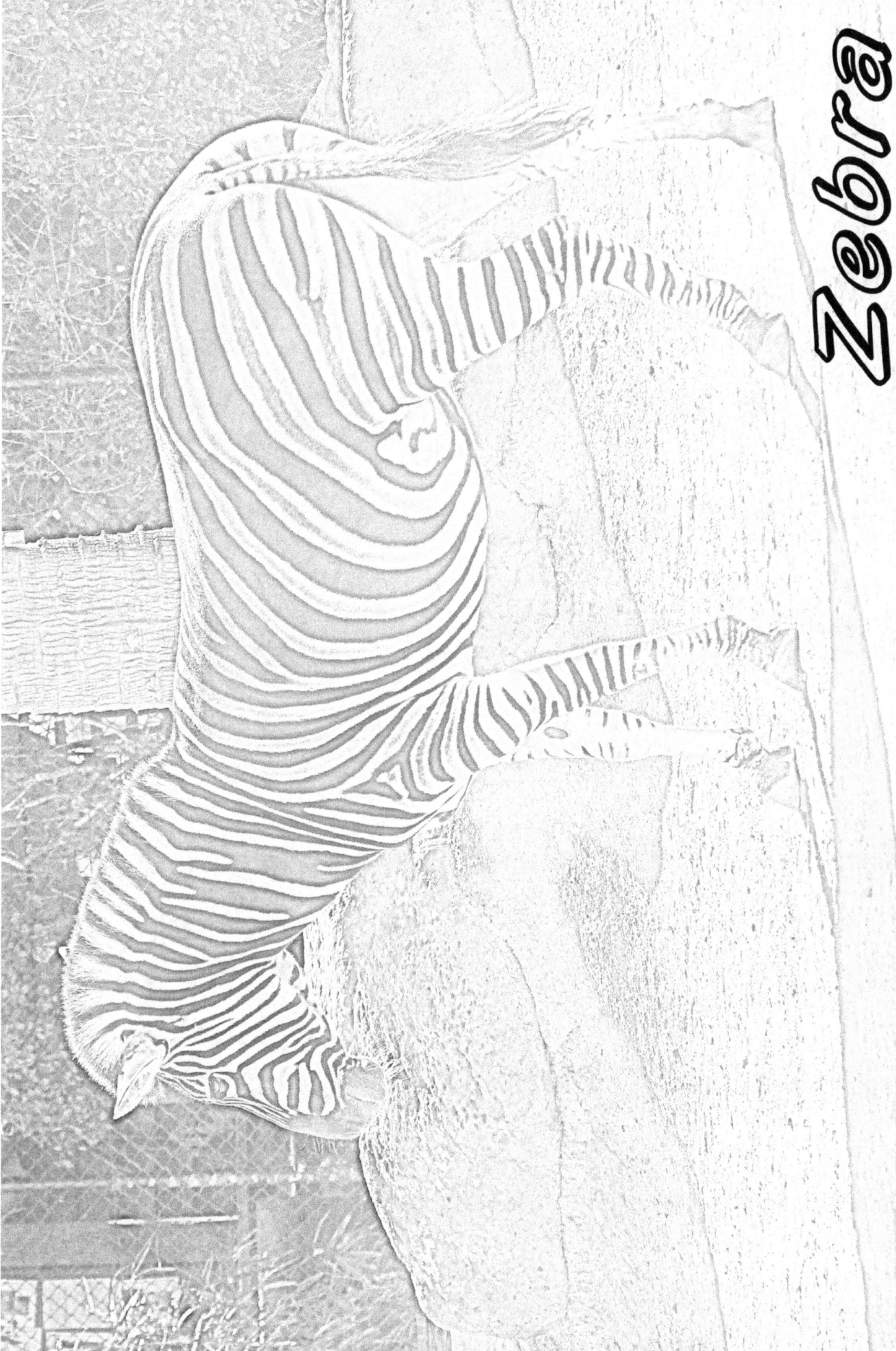

Zebra

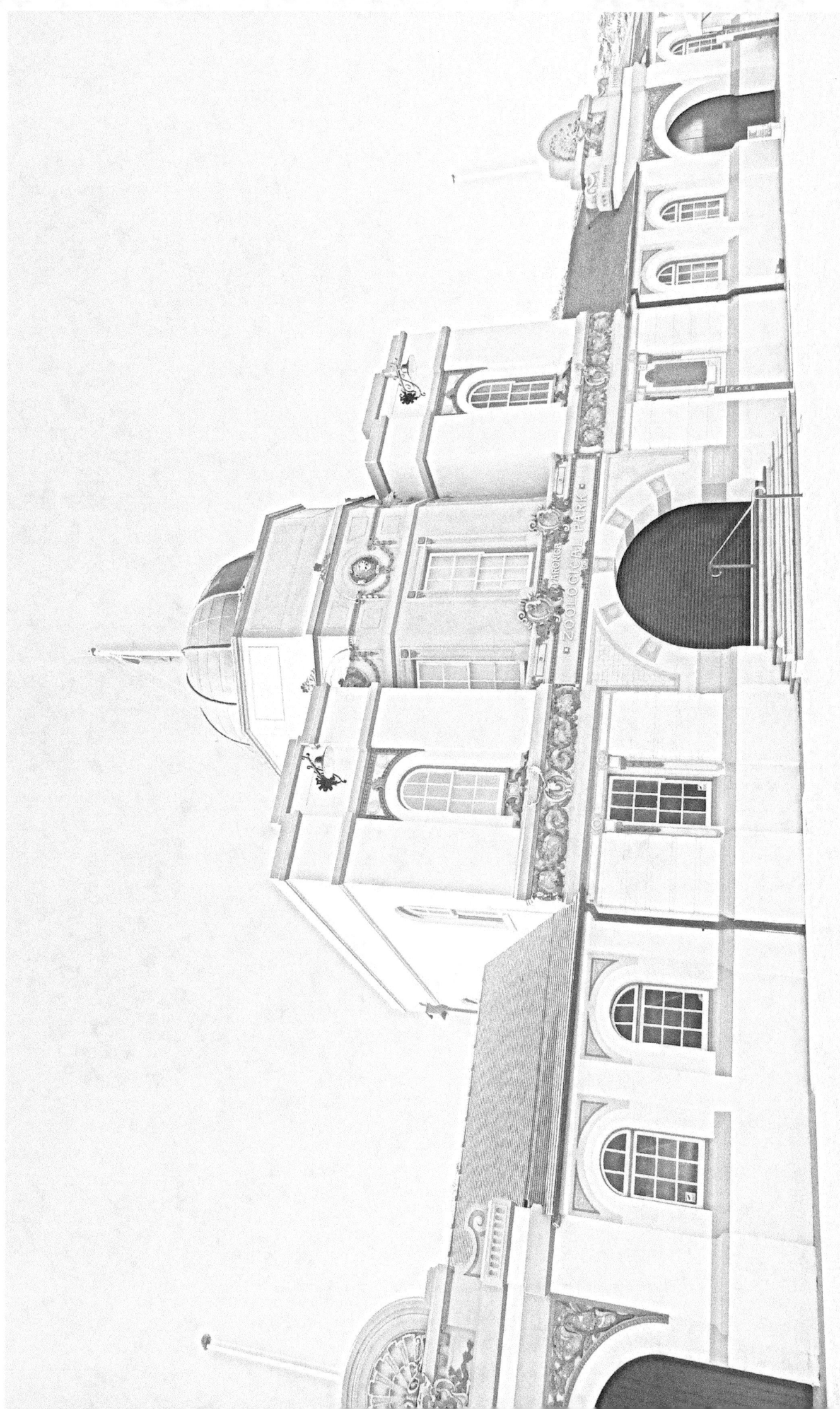

www.ingramcontent.com/pod-product-compliance
Lightning Source LLC
Chambersburg PA
CBHW081051180526
45170CB00005B/1764